COUPLE'S BUCKET LIST

COUPLE'S BUCKET LIST

101

FUN, ENGAGING DATING IDEAS

DR. CAROL MORGAN

ILLUSTRATIONS BY STUDIO MUTI

R

ROCKRIDGE
PRESS

Interior and Cover Designer: Diana Haas
Art Producer: Hannah Dickerson
Editor: Eun H. Jeong
Production Editor: Rachel Taenzler
Production Manager: Martin Worthington

Illustrations © 2021 Studio Muti

ISBN: Print 978-1-64876-823-1 | eBook 978-1-64876-824-8
R1

To Joe. I waited a long time to find you,
and you were worth the wait. I'm excited to see what
the rest of our lives has in store for us.

I love you madly.

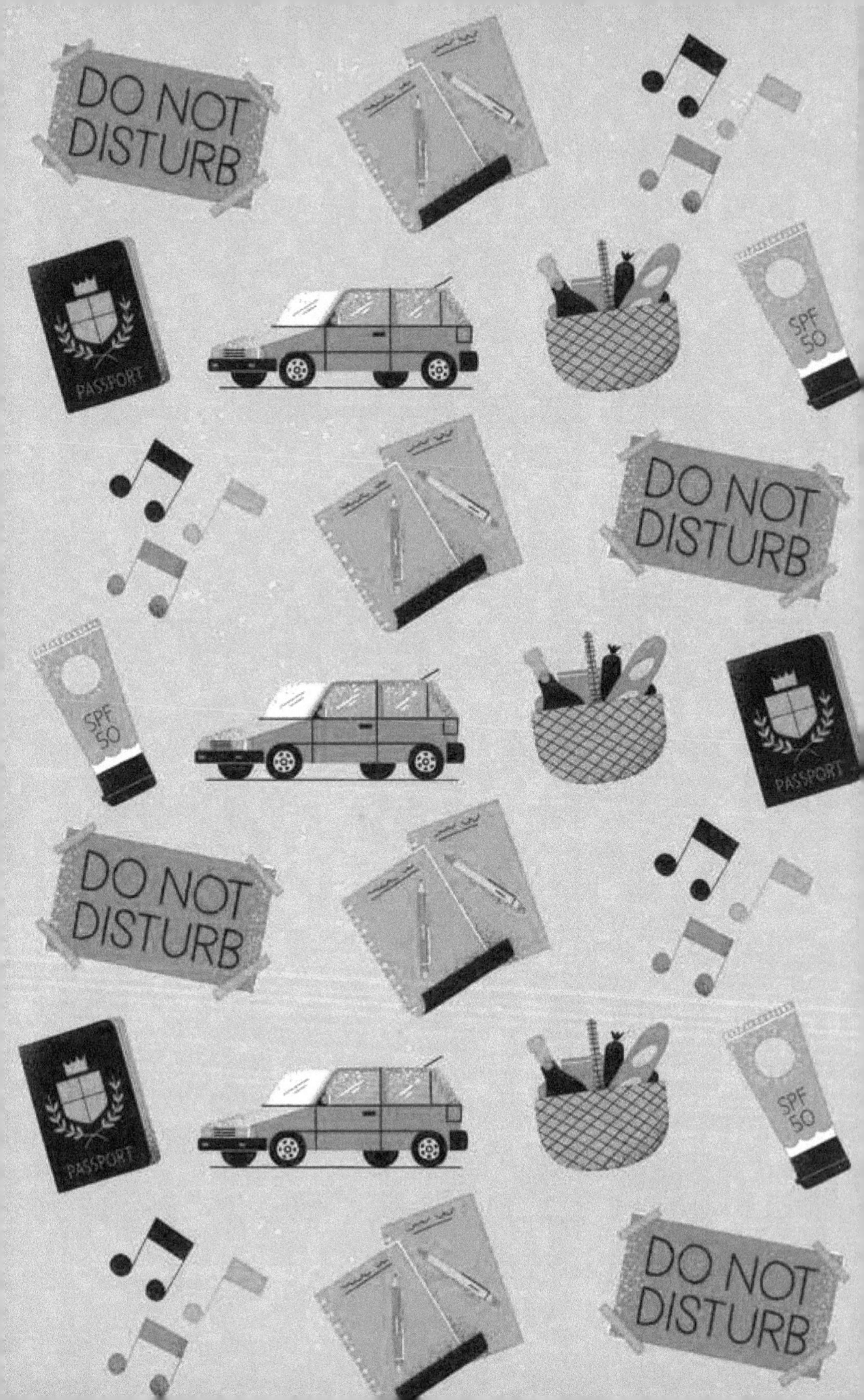
DO NOT DISTURB
PASSPORT
SPF 50

CONTENTS

INTRODUCTION

Hi, my name is Dr. Carol Morgan, and I have a PhD in Gender & Interpersonal Communication. I have been a professor at Wright State University since 1999, and I have taught thousands of people how to have happy, healthy romantic relationships.

In addition to my work as a teacher, I am a dating and relationship coach, speaker, and writer. I have taught life-changing relationship strategies in classrooms, workshops, books, video classes, and on TV and radio. I have seen individuals and couples make great improvements by applying the skills that I teach. I thrive on helping people see new and better ways to experience relationships—and life!

Through my work with couples, I have realized one major thing: The happier and more-committed couples are the ones who make time to date each other, regardless of how long they have been together. Dating is an integral part of relationships that should continue throughout their course. Before marriage, dating helps couples learn more about each other, celebrate or work out differences, and become compatible. After marriage, dating continues that effort and can help couples rediscover things that they may have forgotten over time.

A healthy relationship takes effort, and I know finding creative and interesting things to do together to make each date memorable and meaningful can be hard. That's where this book comes in. Here, I provide 101 great date ideas to help couples build intimacy, discover more about each other, and have lots of fun. Some ideas may seem familiar, but I offer guidance on how to make each date unique to you as a couple. With this list, you will learn how to go on "bucket list" dates—dates that help you make the most of every moment together. And I hope with this list you will find the joy and love of building a healthy and fulfilling relationship.

HOW TO USE THIS BOOK

This book is written for all couples, whether you just started dating or have been together for more than 50 years. We all could use a little inspiration for how to get—or keep—the excitement going in our love lives. The dates in this book are designed to be once-in-a-lifetime experiences that you can set out on to create beautiful memories together (with a variety of budgets).

I strongly encourage you to start with chapter 1 for its insights on dating, relationships, and communication. I also offer advice relevant to all the dates in the following chapters.

The dates are organized by chapter themes to make it easy to find dating inspiration. Think of what you're in the mood to do and how much effort you want to put in. Then, you can open the book and find something exciting within minutes. To help you on your journey, the dates in each chapter are generally listed from the easiest and most accessible to those that are more complex. Some dates, particularly the "super dates," can last longer than a single day or even include international travel. These are special experiences that you'll spend a little more time planning for. Regardless of which dates you choose, this guide will help you get the most out of the quality time you spend together.

In each date, you won't want to miss the Talk about It section that provides conversation starters ranging from light and silly to abstract and introspective. The goal is to help you establish a deeper connection with your partner. I also offer a number of tips on how to modify or plan each date, as well as suggestions on how to get more out of the date. And there is a Speak Your Love Language section that offers suggestions on how you can communicate your love and affection to your partner in the language they are most receptive to.

Ready? Let's get started!

1

HOW TO MAKE DATES GREAT

To get the most out of your dates, you first need to know how to make them great. Good relationships require effort, and that can be part of the fun. This chapter is all about how to maximize your time spent together making memories.

First, I'll start by discussing and defining the concept of "bucket list dating." What exactly does that mean, and how is it different from normal dating? What are some tricks and techniques you can use to create once-in-a-lifetime moments?

Next, I'll go over the concept of love languages. If you've never heard of them, you'll find yourself a little enlightened after you learn how you can use them to better understand yourself and your partner. It is priceless information that will help your relationship grow so much stronger once you understand its importance.

Finally, I'll provide advice for every age and stage of your relationship. We aren't all at the same point in our lives—or our relationships—but whether you've just met or you've been together for decades, there are tips here to help you go on better dates.

WHAT IS BUCKET LIST DATING?

So, what exactly is bucket list dating? You may be familiar with the term "bucket list," which is a list of things one wants to complete before they "kick the bucket." It's meant to be a way to maximize one's time here on earth and have as much fun as possible.

Along those lines, bucket list dating is a way for you and your partner to enhance your time spent together as a couple and make memories that will last a lifetime.

What you won't find here is a book that just lists thrill-seeking things you can do together as a couple. You can find that anywhere. Instead, this book is a detailed guide that will help you actually identify and execute these quintessential activities, from exotic travel to other expensive activities, along with other silly, fun, and simple—but just as valuable—things you can do right in your own home.

Life is meant to be lived to the fullest. We aren't here just to wake up each day, go to work, come home, and rinse and repeat. We need to deeply connect with our loved ones and find enjoyment along the way.

Too often, the daily grind gets in the way of our creativity and inspiration for seizing the day and putting passion into our relationships. That is what this book will give back to you: excitement, fun, and opportunities for connection that you can turn to for decades to come.

YOUR LOVE LANGUAGE

Dr. Gary Chapman is a marriage counselor who has worked with couples for many decades. After years in his practice, he began to notice a particularly troubling pattern: Most people that he worked with did not recognize that their partners actually loved them.

You might say that's understandable, since these couples were going to therapy. But Dr. Chapman also observed that different people express their love differently. And in many cases in his practice, one partner simply was not expressing their love in a way the other recognized. That meant the other partner felt unloved and neglected, leading to tension in their marriage.

This led Dr. Chapman to create what he calls the five love languages: five primary ways people express love and want to receive love. He argued that couples who don't understand each other's love languages may face challenges in their partnership.

The five love languages are: (1) receiving gifts, (2) acts of service, (3) physical touch, (4) words of affirmation, and (5) quality time. Since this book is all about spending quality time together, let's take an in-depth look at the other four love languages first.

RECEIVING GIFTS

Some people really enjoy receiving gifts from other people. It could be a rose, or it could be a big vacation to Hawaii. It could even just be something practical that they want or need, like a new hammer or frying pan. Regardless of what it is, a gift makes those whose love language is receiving gifts feel loved.

But if someone doesn't see the value in gift giving, they might not give their partner anything, even if their partner's love language is receiving gifts. As a result, their partner might not feel loved. Perhaps if they knew that their partner wanted to receive gifts, they would give them. But not having that knowledge can drive a wedge between two people.

ACTS OF SERVICE

An "act of service" is something nice you do for someone else that they either wanted or needed to be done. Unfortunately, sometimes acts of service are not necessarily seen as an expression of love by the partner on the receiving end.

For example, let's say someone washes and details their partner's car. This person believes they are showing their love by keeping their partner's car clean and looking its best. But if their partner doesn't care as much about the cleanliness of their car, they might just be thinking, "Why are they washing my car?"

A more obvious act of service could be giving your partner a massage after a long day at work. This might seem more loving than washing a car, but both qualify as acts of service. Whether these actions are interpreted as expressions of love depends on each partner's outlook.

PHYSICAL TOUCH

This love language is exactly what it sounds like—physically touching your partner. A touch could be as simple as a hug or kiss goodbye on the way to work. It could also be holding hands while walking or cuddling together on the couch while watching a movie. All of this shows that you love your partner enough to touch them.

The language of touch can also involve sexual intimacy. This is an important part of a romantic relationship. While everyone has their own levels of need for sexual activity, many people do not feel loved if there is a lack of sexual interaction in their relationship. This can become a problem if partners have mismatched sex drives. One may feel rejected from the lack of touch, while the other may not have any idea their partner feels that way.

WORDS OF AFFIRMATION

Words of affirmation are one of the more obvious signs of love for many people. This love language involves saying nice things to your partner. It could be a compliment on their outfit, a comment about how smart they are, or an affirmation that you are proud of them.

For people who love receiving words of affirmation, it's also important to actually hear the words "I love you." If they don't hear their partner say these words, they think their partner doesn't actually love them. It could even be important *how* the person says it. A quick "Love ya, bye!" at the end of every phone call might not seem genuine or heartfelt enough.

WHAT'S YOUR LOVE LANGUAGE?

Do you know your love language? Maybe after reading the descriptions of each language, you immediately recognized yours. But then again, maybe you didn't. (And you can actually have more than one love language!)

If you are still unsure what your love language is, that's okay. There are plenty of tests and quizzes on the Internet that you can use to help find yours and your partner's. Once you know each other's love languages, you can start communicating to each other what makes you feel loved and appreciated.

Before you take an online test, here are a few quick questions to ponder that can help you uncover your love language:

1. Do you like it when your partner notices something you're interested in when you are shopping and buys it for you? (Gifts)

2. Do you like it when your partner comes home from work with a little surprise for you, like a bottle of wine or some candy? (Gifts)

3. Do you enjoy giving your partner a massage? (Service)

4. Do you feel good when you help your partner do something that is difficult for them? (Service)

5. Do you like to hear your partner say things like, "I don't know what I would do without you?" (Words)

6. Do you like it when your partner tells you how attractive you are and gives you compliments? (Words)

7. Do you like giving and receiving hugs on a regular basis? (Touch)

8. Do you like it when your partner holds you in bed? (Touch)

9. Do you like going on trips with just your partner as much as possible? (Time)

10. Do you like it when your partner prefers to spend time with you instead of going out with their friends? (Time)

SPEAK YOUR LOVE LANGUAGE

Healthy communication in a relationship is so important. However, many people think that their partner should instinctively know what they want and need without ever being told directly. This isn't very realistic for most people.

In a relationship, it's important to discover both of your love languages and to communicate them to each other. Once you know each other's love languages, you can speak to your partner in their language and strive to meet each other's needs more fully for a healthy and fulfilling relationship.

ADVICE FOR EVERY AGE AND STAGE

Every couple goes through different phases in their relationship. While no two couples have the exact same needs or trajectory, throughout my career I have discovered some basic best practices for better dates that cover various general stages of relationships. While I divide these tips by stage, most of them will help you regardless of which phase of your relationship you happen to be in—whether you just met each other, have been married over 50 years, or are anywhere along that spectrum.

ADVICE FOR COUPLES WHO JUST MET

TIP NO. 1

Keep your dates inexpensive yet enjoyable. You have no idea if this person is going to be someone you are compatible with, so keep your dates simple, like having coffee or lunch. This is a great way to get to know a stranger because it doesn't require either of you to invest too much time or money into a relationship you are not sure about yet.

TIP NO. 2

Ask personal questions on your dates. Some people are afraid to ask personal questions or don't like answering them. But how else are you going to get to know someone if you don't talk about yourselves? You might discover something you really like (or dislike). Asking questions is the only way to find out.

TIP NO. 3

Be respectful of each other by scheduling dates ahead of time (and not rescheduling or canceling). You want to treat your date the way you would want to be treated, so be very mindful of not wasting their time. Don't accept bad behavior from them, either.

TIP NO. 4

Set emotional boundaries. Dating someone can feel exciting and new, but be sure to set and respect your emotional boundaries. Healthy boundaries protect you from letting someone else's feelings dictate your own and from sacrificing your own needs to provide for and please another. At the end of the day, remember to protect your sense of self and self-esteem: You are still your own person.

TIP NO. 5

Be honest and up-front about what you want. You need to get clear about who and what you are looking for. Do you want to date casually? Are you looking for a long-term relationship? Marriage? If you don't know, be honest about that to yourself and your partner. Mutual honesty is key to the foundation of a relationship at any stage.

ADVICE FOR COUPLES WHO ARE GETTING SERIOUS

TIP NO. 1

When planning your dates, try to do things you both enjoy. Activities can involve things you both like to do or values that you share. Try to discover activities that you enjoy doing *together*, because that will give you insight into whether or not you are compatible in the long run.

TIP NO. 2

On your dates, engage in some deep conversation. Some people will advise you to keep your discussions light and stay away from topics like politics or religion. But avoiding topics that express your core beliefs doesn't help you assess whether or not you are right for each other. Have the heavy conversations, and remember to keep an open mind and be understanding of what is shared.

TIP NO. 3

Make your dates longer and more meaningful. Since you have both reached the point where you think this could turn into a committed (and maybe even long-term) relationship, it's wise to put more effort into every date. It shows that you are definitely more serious about each other.

TIP NO. 4

Define the relationship. Too many couples don't officially talk about the status of their relationship. One person might think they are in an exclusive relationship, while the other one doesn't. It's important that you are both on the same page, so have an honest discussion about where you both see things going.

TIP NO. 5

Discuss your expectations for a long-term relationship. Depending on your age, there are various important discussions that should be had. If you're eager to start a family soon, you need to be sure your partner is, too; otherwise, you could both be set up for disappointment down the road. There are many other long-term factors that should be discussed, so make sure you are communicating your expectations to each other.

ADVICE FOR COUPLES IN LONG-TERM RELATIONSHIPS

TIP NO. 1

Remember that *every* date doesn't have to be elaborate or expensive. Since you've made it to the point of being together in a long-term, committed relationship, the dates can "relax" a little. But that is only because you are probably seeing each other a lot more (or even living together). You can find plenty of enjoyment in simplicity or everyday moments.

TIP NO. 2

On the other hand, you now *can* make dates elaborate and expensive if you want to. This is the stage where you can go on fun vacations and adventures together. Since you are a solid couple now, you might even have merged finances, so you can definitely make some great memories doing some exotic things.

TIP NO. 3

Don't forget to "date" each other on a regular basis. It's too easy to get distracted by life and forget that you should put effort into your relationship. Don't get complacent or lazy! If possible, you should go out on a date at least once a week so that you can stay connected long-term.

TIP NO. 4

Put your partner's needs at least equal to, if not before, your own. Be generous with your partner in considering their needs and love language. Sharing your needs might not come naturally to you or your partner, so it's important to lovingly ask them what it is they need and want from you and the relationship. Then, take action to make your partner happy, and they will naturally do the same for you.

TIP NO. 5

Never stop showing love and appreciation. It's easy to take each other for granted after being together for a long time. But don't let it get to that point: Show your partner you love and appreciate them every single day!

BEING YOUR BEST DATE

As the saying goes: "It takes two to tango." In other words, both of you need to put in 100 percent effort on your dates in order for them to be successful. Neither of you can carry the relationship on your own shoulders, so you need to work as a team!

Remember to be mindful, focused, and connected to each other on dates. Put your phones away and look into each other's eyes when you speak. Paraphrase your partner's thoughts and feelings back to them so that they know you are really listening. Hold each other's hands so that you can become more physically intimate. Good communication, both verbal and nonverbal, is essential to making a relationship work, so be present and show your partner that your whole focus is on them.

Sometimes, you get so caught up in life's details that you don't always enjoy the moment. You miss the fun and excitement of being together— just the two of you! So, don't talk about the kids, or work, or your financial woes. Instead, get creative and have fun with your conversation. *Do aliens really exist? What would we do if we won $100,000,000 in the lottery? Would we stay in a haunted house if we had the chance?*

Dates are an opportunity to either stay connected or reconnect if you feel like you have drifted apart. The goal is to not become one of those couples who forget why they fell in love. That's why dates are so vitally important to truly living happily ever after. Never underestimate the power of a great date!

DO NOT DISTURB
PASSPORT
SPF 50
DO NOT DISTURB
SPF 50
PASSPORT
DO NOT DISTURB
PASSPORT
SPF 50
DO NOT DISTURB

2

TRAVEL & ADVENTURE

Let's start the dates off with a bang, shall we? Travel and adventure are probably what a lot of people think of when they hear the term "bucket list." Such experiences allow you to explore new places, meet new people, and do things you don't normally do. Travel and adventure are already fun and exhilarating, but when you travel with your partner on a date, it can become even more meaningful and memorable, truly turning into a once-in-a-lifetime experience.

I love excitement, but I admit that sometimes I have to push outside of my comfort zone in order to really get the full experience. For example, a couple of years ago, my partner and I decided to go parasailing. It sounded like a great idea . . . until I saw how high you go. I almost didn't go through with it, but I'm happy I did because it was an adventure to remember.

This is a great example of something you should keep in mind. If you are not a risk-taker, then maybe do some research before you go adventuring. That way, you will know exactly what to expect. But remember: Just because something seems a little nerve-racking doesn't mean you shouldn't do it. Try to have an open mind and be brave; you definitely won't regret it.

So, are you up for some crazy and memorable dates you can talk about for years to come?

Ready, set . . . let's go!

1 SPOOKY DATING

What could be spookier and more exciting than an actual ghost tour? There are many cities that offer tours of haunted areas. Search for options online, decide which one you want to do, and make a plan.

TIPS

- Look around and see if you can spot any paranormal phenomena, such as orbs, shadows, or a strange feeling or sound.
- Ask the tour guide to tell you specific stories of other people who have had experiences with creepy ghosts or goblins.
- After the ghost tour, try to find a real haunted house to visit or a hotel for an overnight stay.

TALK ABOUT IT

Talk to your partner about what their beliefs are, if any, in an afterlife. Do they believe in ghosts? If so, why do they think they are still earthbound? Would they be scared to have an encounter with a ghost?

SPEAK YOUR LOVE LANGUAGE

You can hold tight to each other during the tour and talk about what you find so courageous in each other. Ask your partner what would make them feel the most loved during this kind of "scary" date.

MAKE THE MOST OF IT

Do some research ahead of time to see if you can learn more about the history of the places you are going to visit on the ghost tour. Swap stories about your encounters with paranormal activity (if you have had any).

2 CHILDHOOD TIME MACHINE

Pretend that you have a time machine, and jump back into your childhood. You can learn more about how each of you grew up. Plus, it's fun and exciting to act like a kid again.

TIPS

- Bring your partner back to one of the schools you attended as a child. If you are allowed inside, walk around the halls and talk about the memories.
- Drive to the home where you grew up. If your parents don't live there anymore, why not knock on the door and politely ask if you could get a tour?
- If you both live too far from your old schools or homes, try going to an empty playground and pretending that you are kids again.

TALK ABOUT IT

Before you embark on this date, make a list of the best memories from your childhood. Then, share your lists with each other. Figure out how you can fit these memories into your trip back in time. During the date, ask each other questions about your childhoods and how you each have grown from your experiences.

SPEAK YOUR LOVE LANGUAGE

Hold hands as you walk around and explore the locations of your childhood, give a little nostalgic gift from the past, or praise each other for how proud you are of your pasts.

MAKE THE MOST OF IT

Dig up some memorabilia from your youth to show your partner. It could be an old yearbook, a school uniform, or notes you passed to your friends.

BIGGEST, FASTEST, TALLEST, BESTEST!

Have you ever wanted to explore the biggest, smallest, oldest, newest, tallest, shortest, fastest, or slowest . . . anything? That's called a "superlative," and it might take a little bit of research on your part, but you can find and explore such extreme places on dates. This could be in your town, your state, your country, or somewhere on the other side of the world—whatever is within your means and schedule.

TIPS

- Once you pinpoint what kinds of things you want to explore, search the Internet and map out a trip. This allows you to efficiently see as many sites as possible in a single trip.
- If you don't have the time or energy to plan the experience yourself, find a guided tour that will make the date easy for you.

TALK ABOUT IT

Talk about the kinds of "extremes" you have experienced, or would like to experience, in your lives. It could be something completely outrageous like visiting Mars someday or something more earthbound like riding the tallest, fastest roller coaster in the world.

SPEAK YOUR LOVE LANGUAGE

If you experience something intense, like the roller coaster mentioned above, you can hold each other's hands and squeeze tight if you need to. Or, instead of going on a trip at all, you could have a friendly competition over who loves each other the most—and why. This is consistent with the theme of superlatives and will make both of you feel especially beloved.

MAKE THE MOST OF IT

After visiting one set of superlatives, go visit the exact opposites for another date!

TAKE A SCENIC RIDE

While horseback riding may or may not seem adventurous to some people, you can make it a special experience with a little planning. Find a unique place, either locally or while on vacation, and take your horse for a ride in the great outdoors.

TIPS

- One of the most romantic places to ride on horseback is on a beach. You've seen it in the movies, so why not try it for yourself? Most tropical places offer beach horseback rides.
- If you're not up for the beach, then try a ride through the mountains or rocky hills. That can be just as romantic as the ocean and sand.
- Just for fun, go out and buy some cowboy/cowgirl clothes to wear on the ride. Dressing the part will add to your experience (and it's just plain fun).

TALK ABOUT IT

Talk about your feelings toward animals. What do you like about them? Would you like to own any exotic animals if you could? Why or why not?

SPEAK YOUR LOVE LANGUAGE

Help each other up and down off the horses. If you're comfortable and riding side by side, hold hands on the horses for a few minutes. Buy each other cowboy hats or a keepsake to commemorate the date.

MAKE THE MOST OF IT

Plan a "western" vacation at a dude ranch. You can be each other's own cowboy and cowgirl in an immersive trip riding horseback through canyons, mountain ranges, river gorges, or whatever ranch environment you choose.

5 ZIP THROUGH THE AIR

Zip-lining is an extreme activity that can be absolutely exhilarating! And it's not hard to find a place to do it. Whether you want to stay close to home or go on a tropical vacation, you can find a place to go zip-lining pretty much anywhere.

TIPS

- Research the different options within your budget and comfort zone. Some zip-lining places are long, high, and scary. Others are relatively tame in comparison.
- Different locations offer different scenery. Decide on what kind you would like to see while zip-lining.
- See if you can find a place that will take videos or pictures of you while you zip-line. Having the experience recorded forever will make for a nice keepsake.

TALK ABOUT IT

Zip-lining can make you feel like you are flying through the air. Ask each other about the places you would visit if you were able to fly anywhere.

SPEAK YOUR LOVE LANGUAGE

Zip-lining can be scary, so hold each other's hands on the way up, and hug each other until you have to jump off the ledge. Buy or make each other commemorative shirts that you can wear to remember your experience.

MAKE THE MOST OF IT

Ask your partner to name five things they would *never* do and five things they *have* to do before they die. Write down both of your responses and hang that piece of paper somewhere prominent in your home. Challenge each other to make a plan to cross each one off the list.

6 WINTERTIME ROMANCE

Winter can be long and lonely because it's difficult to find outdoor activities, especially if it's not snowing where you live. But if you can find snow, going skiing or snowboarding is a great way to be active during those cold months. If you've never done it before, it's also a fun way to bond.

TIPS

- Find a ski slope close to home if you can. Even if it's not snowing (or not even that cold), many of these places produce their own snow, so you can go any time during winter.
- Take ski or snowboard lessons before you hit the big slopes. This will help improve your skills and keep you safe, and it will probably produce some laughs along the way, too.
- You can also try dogsledding or snowmobiling if you have already gone skiing and snowboarding.

TALK ABOUT IT

Talk about your favorite childhood winter memories. What was the biggest snowfall year you remember? Did you go sledding with your parents? Are you an expert at making a snowman?

SPEAK YOUR LOVE LANGUAGE

Skiing or snowboarding can offer the opportunity to perform acts of service, as you both may need to help each other learn the necessary skills. Use words of encouragement to let your partner know how much you support them and care.

MAKE THE MOST OF IT

Don't forget to take breaks and connect in the lodge over some hot chocolate or cocktails. Be safe and reserve the cocktails for *after* you are done skiing for the day.

EXTREME DATING

If you both enjoy extreme sports, why not try skydiving or bungee jumping? These activities are not for the faint of heart, so you both need to make sure you have a great sense of adventure (and a good heart!) before you try them.

TIPS

- Research testimonies and/or video footage of people actually going skydiving or bungee jumping before you do it. You'll get a better sense of what the activity entails and if it's right for you.
- Choose a place that will let you record your adventure. This can be a once-in-a-lifetime experience, and you may want to relive your bravery and show it to friends.
- Challenge each other and ask what fears you are confronting with these activities. Are you afraid of free-falling? What concerns fill your mind?

TALK ABOUT IT

This is a great opportunity to open a deep discussion about your greatest fears in general—not just about skydiving or bungee jumping.

SPEAK YOUR LOVE LANGUAGE

Extreme activities can be great bonding experiences for a couple. They can feel like life-or-death situations as you face your fears together. Make and give each other commemorative gifts. Encourage each other with loving words.

MAKE THE MOST OF IT

Write down your "last words" and give them to each other. This is just for fun, since this date can be scary for some people. You can have an open conversation after reading what you would say to each other if this was your last day on earth.

8 AQUATIC ADVENTURES

Commune with nature and your animal friends by diving into the ocean together. Swim alongside dolphins or dive deep into the sea to discover all the marine life we never get a chance to see on land.

TIPS

- Research the marine life of your destination ahead of time so that you know what to look for when scuba diving.
- Choose a tropical location such as Hawaii or the Bahamas, and plan an unforgettable vacation with a focus on water activities.
- If on a budget, try visiting an aquarium where you can study and touch sea creatures without having to break the bank.

TALK ABOUT IT

What do you love most about the ocean and marine life? Talk about what you are most excited to see in the water. Since scuba diving involves going deep into the ocean, talk about any fears of water you might have (or had as a child).

SPEAK YOUR LOVE LANGUAGE

You are both going to be in swimsuits, so take the opportunity to flirt with your partner with a loving touch—maybe a tap on their backside—or a compliment on how hot and sexy they look. Surprise your partner with the gift of a new swimsuit; a tropical vacation is a great opportunity to show it off.

MAKE THE MOST OF IT

Plan an entire vacation centered around water activities. There is much more that you can do beyond swimming with dolphins and scuba diving. You can ride Jet Skis, rent a boat, or go parasailing.

9 A FROZEN CATCH FOR TWO

Standing on a frozen lake underneath a blue sky, enjoying the stillness on the ice—ice fishing can be a fun, restorative, and even meditative experience. Prepare to make a day of it, and be sure to dress warmly!

TIPS

- Safety is the number-one concern. Unless you have experience with checking the ice for thickness and the necessary equipment for ice fishing, you'll want to pay for an ice fishing tour with a licensed guide and all the gear included.
- Make time to take in everything around you. Hold your partner's hand and share a moment of gratitude.
- Your tour will probably include an ice hut and cooking equipment, so you can try your hand at cooking some of your freshly caught fish together. Or you can wait until you get home to cook your catch and extend your date into the evening.

TALK ABOUT IT

Since fishing involves patience, discuss your levels of patience with other people and life in general.

SPEAK YOUR LOVE LANGUAGE

Check in to be sure your partner is warm and having fun. Perform acts of service to help your partner when you can, like preparing hot chocolate, checking your lines, or telling some jokes to pass the time.

MAKE THE MOST OF IT

If you have the financial means, why not turn this into a trip to see the northern lights in Norway? You can do multiple once-in-a-lifetime activities: seeing the lights, fjords, museums, and attractions of Norway and doing some ice fishing surrounded by breathtaking natural beauty.

HEALING ENERGY OF VORTICES

Many people have never heard of an energy vortex (swirling center of spiritual energy). There are many in Sedona, Arizona, and reportedly some very mystical things can happen there. While in Sedona, the Grand Canyon is also a must-see.

TIPS

- Drive through the red rocks of Sedona and go to Boynton Canyon, one of the most powerful energy vortex sites. Sit among the majestic rocks and try some meditation.
- Take a helicopter ride in the Grand Canyon for an unforgettable experience.
- If you're up for even more adventure, take a donkey ride down the side of the Grand Canyon or go whitewater rafting in the Colorado River.

TALK ABOUT IT

Ask each other questions about energy vortices and whether or not you believe in the mysticism behind them. You could do some research together and discover how they got there and how the Grand Canyon was formed.

SPEAK YOUR LOVE LANGUAGE

If you are hiking and meditating in Boynton Canyon, remember to hold hands and connect your energy. In the rocky terrain, you can show your love by making sure you both are safe and secure during your hikes. Encourage each other if you encounter a difficult portion of a hike, and be of service to your partner if they need help.

MAKE THE MOST OF IT

Sedona is known to have a community of psychics and energy healers. Try visiting one and find out if they can see into your future or heal a physical ailment you may have.

UNDERGROUND ESCAPADE

Whether you opt for a local cave, a cavern with a guided tour, or a far-flung destination like the Lascaux cave in France, this date will be an adventure.

TIPS

- Regardless of which type of adventure you choose, plan ahead to ensure you're properly equipped for your trip. If there is a local cave near you frequented by spelunkers (people who explore caves), you may want to check out the National Speleological Society to find a meetup group. For added safety, it helps to go spelunking in groups.
- Make this a destination date and travel to France to see the Lascaux cave paintings. These Paleolithic paintings are around 20,000 years old, and viewing them is a once-in-a-lifetime experience. For conservation reasons the original cave is closed to visitors, but you can take a tour of a complete replica of the cave close by.

TALK ABOUT IT

Did your family go on vacations, and if so, what kind? Is there anything holding you back from cave exploration, like a fear of the dark or enclosed spaces?

SPEAK YOUR LOVE LANGUAGE

Help each other down slippery steps, through narrow passages, and across uneven footing. If your partner is nervous, compliment them on their bravery.

MAKE THE MOST OF IT

Take a hike around the area of the cave to appreciate the natural beauty of your surroundings. If you decide to make this a destination date, do a little research to find additional must-see places near your destination. For example, there are more than 150 prehistoric sites in the Lascaux area.

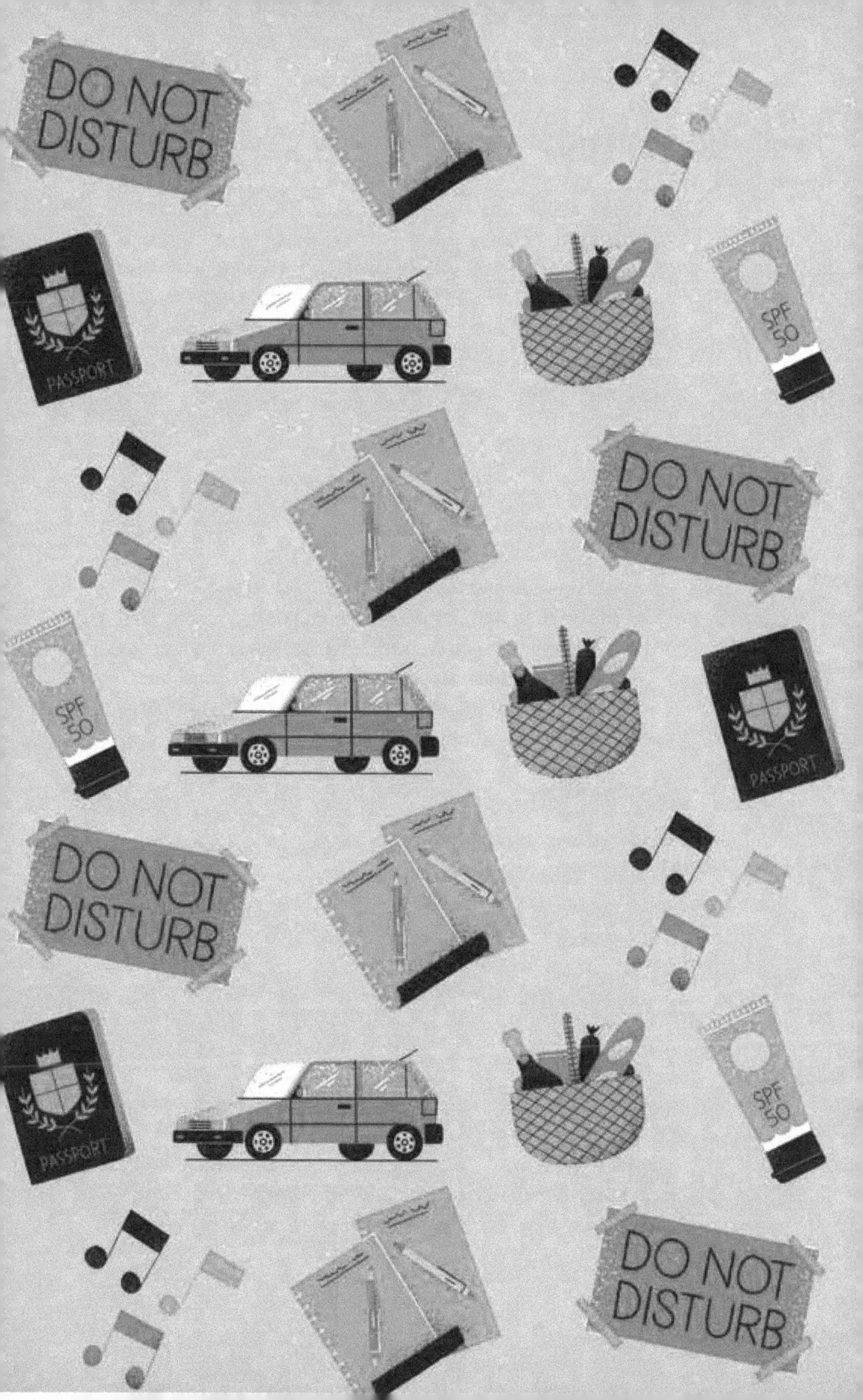
DO NOT DISTURB
PASSPORT
SPF 50

SUPER DATE
EXPLORE ANCIENT RUINS

Machu Picchu is one of the New Seven Wonders of the World. Located on top of a mountain range in Peru, it is one of the most well-preserved Incan cities, an example of Incan masonry that has stood the test of time. Archaeologists believe that Machu Picchu was constructed for an Incan emperor in the mid-1400s CE. Who better to see an ancient architectural marvel with than your partner?

TIPS

- Take a tour of the archaeological site so that you don't miss anything. You'll learn a lot of facts about Machu Picchu when guided by an expert.
- Be adventurous and explore on your own. Make sure you visit the Temple of the Sun and the Intihuatana stone.
- Try to stay in a hotel in Aguas Calientes, the closest access point to the historical site of Machu Picchu. Proximity will help maximize your time and afford you a glorious view for your romantic vacation.

TALK ABOUT IT

There are many other wonders in the world, like the Great Pyramid of Giza in Egypt and Stonehenge in England. Do you believe people from ancient times built them, or do you believe extraterrestrial theories? A zany question could lead to an unforgettable conversation. If you could time travel back to one of those times, would you do it? Why or why not?

SPEAK YOUR LOVE LANGUAGE

Visit one of the thermal baths near Aguas Calientes and relax in each other's arms. Visit the local market and buy your partner a unique gift to commemorate the time you shared together at this magical place. Rub your partner's feet or shoulders after a long day of walking and climbing.

MAKE THE MOST OF IT

Depending on your budget, time, and preferences, you could expand this trip into a guided tour all around Peru instead of or in addition to a tour of the historical site of Machu Picchu. Or you could go your own way if you prefer to be independent explorers—just make sure you plan ahead so that you don't miss any highlights on this romantic adventure.

3

ALL ABOUT US

This chapter is all about dates that focus on the two of you. You'll learn more about each other, deepen your connection, and prioritize your relationship. You will also create, or revive, more romance in your lives.

In the beginning of a relationship, romance comes naturally. You are both infatuated, and that feeling is like a high that seems like it will never end. But the longer you are together, the more you might find that life gets in the way of romance. Thankfully, it doesn't have to! You can choose to stay romantic and focus on the bond between the two of you in order to build a lasting love.

Keep in mind that romance isn't just about the candles, flowers, and candy. You can be romantic in so many different ways, such as going on the bucket list dates in this chapter, which are designed to celebrate the two of you. Romance creates good memories. And when you challenge yourself to do something that you've always wanted to do, something new, and/or something outside of your comfort zone, the shared memories that you form lead to stronger relationships and deeper connections with your partner.

I've seen both sides of the relationship coin. I've been in relationships where we let the romance between us slip away, and as a result, the whole relationship faded away, too. I've also been in relationships where we both put in equal effort to keep our romance alive. And I am here to tell you: That is key to making a relationship great!

LOVE LETTERS

Whether you're starting out in a new relationship or you've been together for a long time, communicating how you feel about each other is paramount. Take the time to reflect on your affection for your partner by writing them a love letter.

TIPS

- Reflect on at least three of your favorite memories of your partner and/or your relationship. Share why these memories are your favorites.
- Write at least 10 things you like about your partner. It could be their beautiful eyes, their outgoing personality, or their gentle nature.
- Tell your partner what your hopes and dreams are for the two of you as a couple. What does your future look like in your heart and mind?

TALK ABOUT IT

Have a discussion about what makes your partner unique to you from anyone else you've ever dated. Have them do the same with you.

SPEAK YOUR LOVE LANGUAGE

This date lends itself perfectly to sharing and receiving words of affirmation. You can also snuggle up to each other on the couch and read your love letters out loud. Follow it up with a make-out session if the mood takes you!

MAKE THE MOST OF IT

Make your love letters as intentional and detailed as you possibly can. This is an opportunity to put your heart and soul onto the page for your partner to read and reread. Make an agreement to write new letters at least once a year (and perhaps on your anniversary or another special occasion).

14 RELAXATION FOR TWO

Massages are the perfect way to unwind and let all the details of life that are stressing you out melt away. A couple's massage delivers all of this in an intimate bonding experience. Many massage therapists offer couple's massage and even use romantic lights and music to set the scene for your date.

TIPS

- Find massage therapists who regularly perform couple's massages. They will know how to help make the experience romantic for you so that you hardly have to do any of the work.
- Plan something romantic for after the massage—perhaps a picnic in a park or a candlelit dinner at home.

TALK ABOUT IT

Since massages are all about relaxation, before you go, talk about what stresses you out the most in life. Is it your job? The kids? Your finances? Too often, people bottle these stresses inside their head and don't talk to their partner about them. Sharing your worries with each other will help you decompress and let go even more.

SPEAK YOUR LOVE LANGUAGE

Ask the massage therapists to put your massage tables close enough together that you can hold hands during your session. Compliment your partner on how attractive you think they are when they are half naked. Buy your partner a sexy robe to wear during the massage; this can also be a way to remember your date.

MAKE THE MOST OF IT

Bring scented oils and ask the massage therapists to use them on both of you. Make a romantic playlist to be played during your session to personalize your experience even more.

15 OPEN HOUSE FOR AN OPEN HEART

If you're in the market for a new house or condominium, or even just interested in architecture and interior design, why not make touring some open houses into a date? It's a fun way to fantasize about your next home and get some great ideas.

TIPS

- Even if you're not looking to buy a new home, it can be fun to explore homes for sale to get some new decorating tips.
- Do your research ahead of time and make a plan. You'll avoid driving around aimlessly looking for an open house, and you may be able to visit several open houses in one date.
- Go see some dream houses: the types of homes you've always wanted to live in but are maybe outside of your reach.

TALK ABOUT IT

Talk about what kinds of features are must-haves in your next home. Do you need an open floor plan? How many bedrooms and bathrooms? Do you prefer old, historical houses? Not only is it fun to talk about these kinds of things, but these discussions can also clarify your goals for the future.

SPEAK YOUR LOVE LANGUAGE

Even if you are not looking for a future home, why not buy each other "housewarming gifts" for your current home(s)? And don't forget to hold hands while you tour the open houses and hold the door for each other.

MAKE THE MOST OF IT

If you fall in love with a certain neighborhood, take a walk together or drive around to look at other houses in the area.

16 FRAME-WORTHY PHOTOS

Get dressed up and capture some romantic photos of you and your partner that you'll want to frame. If you can secure the help of a friend, this date gives you a chance to have photos taken together at a reasonable price (free!).

TIPS

- Try at least three different clothing options: one very formal, one semiformal, and one casual.
- Plan for a variety of shooting locations: the woods, a bridge, at home, the rooftop of a building, or another place that's meaningful to you or makes for a great backdrop for photos.
- Select your favorites together and order prints to display in a collage in your home(s).

TALK ABOUT IT

Since this date is all about taking photos, talk about your school pictures through the years. Which ones were your favorites or the worst? Describe your outfits or pull out your school pictures to show your partner. This could spark a good belly laugh since we often regret the fashion choices of our youth.

SPEAK YOUR LOVE LANGUAGE

Help each other pick out clothes to wear for the photo shoot. During the shoot, make sure you hold each other. You could hold hands or wrap your arms around each other. When the photo shoot is complete, look at the photos together and compliment your partner on how handsome or beautiful they look.

MAKE THE MOST OF IT

Save the most formal clothing for the last photos. Then, after you are done with the session, go out for a fancy dinner dressed like you are attending a black-tie ball.

DIY DATING

Have you always wanted to learn how to cook a gourmet meal? Mix a cocktail? Blow a glass bottle? There are couple's classes available for most anything you can imagine. Pick a class you'd like to take together and make a date out of it.

TIPS

- Brainstorm a list of interests you and your partner share. Make the list as long as you can to find commonalities and choose the right hobby to learn.
- Set a goal and budget. For example, if you want to take a woodworking class, is your goal to do some home improvement? And what are you willing to spend?
- Make sure to pick something you *both* are passionate about learning and doing.

TALK ABOUT IT

Take a look at your brainstorm list and ask each other about the interests that you don't have in common. What intrigues you or your partner about these hobbies? What is holding you back from learning these skills? Are any of them secret career goals?

SPEAK YOUR LOVE LANGUAGE

Compliment and encourage each other as you learn your new skill or hobby. Doing something new that neither of you have any expertise in presents an opportunity for you to be vulnerable and intimate together. If you are taking a class in which you are making something, make it for your partner!

MAKE THE MOST OF IT

You don't have to limit yourselves to just one class. Take a series of classes on the same topic to become experts, or explore new hobbies and skills.

18 JOINT SCRAPBOOKING

Find as many photos of you and your partner as you possibly can, from birth until the present day. If they are old, then scan them or take a picture of them with your phone and print a copy. Arrange all of the photos together chronologically in a scrapbook so that you can see the "evolution of us."

TIPS

- Put pictures of both of you at the same age beside each other to see how you looked at the same phase of life.
- Write funny captions underneath each photo, such as: "What was I thinking with that hairstyle?"
- Pay special attention to the photos taken after you met each other. Take turns writing funny and/or romantic captions or recording memories associated with each one.

TALK ABOUT IT

Ask each other to talk about a favorite memory from the scrapbook. It could be from before you met or a moment you shared together.

SPEAK YOUR LOVE LANGUAGE

Say complimentary or loving things about your partner in your captions. These words will make them feel cherished. You can also try cooking a special dinner for your partner and doing this date by candlelight.

MAKE THE MOST OF IT

Make this a regular date night. Once you have assembled the scrapbook, keep adding to it throughout the years. You don't have to stop at the present day; you can keep it going for your whole lives (but you might need some more scrapbooks!).

19 STAR IN A MUSIC VIDEO

Music videos are fun to watch, but have you ever wanted to star in one? This date is a joint creative venture that could be your debut appearance in a music video. First, each of you should pick a song you would enjoy performing. Then, record yourselves lip-synching to your picks in a few different locations. Commit to your roles, be over-the-top, and embrace your superstardom.

TIPS

- Find a video editing app on your phone or computer that is easy to use. No need to get too complicated. Keep this fun!
- Record two different videos: one for each of your favorite songs.
- Make a romantic video to a classic love ballad and a fun video to an upbeat karaoke song. When you are done, you can both slow dance and fast dance to your masterpieces.

TALK ABOUT IT

List what you think are the top five best music videos of all time. Be ready to defend your picks, and have a friendly "debate" to try to justify why your list is better than your partner's.

SPEAK YOUR LOVE LANGUAGE

Turn the lights down low and hold each other tight as you slow dance to your new romantic video. Whisper loving words into your partner's ear as you sway back and forth.

MAKE THE MOST OF IT

If you both enjoyed this date, keep it in mind for the future. Make each other more music videos for special occasions like birthdays or anniversaries. As time goes by, you'll create a collection of fun videos to enjoy.

ROMANTIC RENOVATION

Many people fantasize about redecorating or updating their house or apartment, so why not make it into a fun date? Depending on your budget, this could be a big renovation or a refresh of one room. Whether or not you live with your partner, this date is definitely a bonding experience because you are working together to improve your partner's or your sanctuary.

TIPS

- Watch home improvement shows (such as *Property Brothers, Flip or Flop,* and *Fixer Upper)* for ideas.
- Go shopping together for art to hang or trinkets to display in your space to give it a new look and feel.
- If you enjoy antiquing, go to antique shops, garage sales, or flea markets to find unique pieces to add to your space.

TALK ABOUT IT

You may not have it in your budget to build a mansion, but it's fun to imagine and talk about! Ask each other what your dream home would be if there were no limitations on your budget. What would it look like? Where would it be located? What special and unique features would it have? A swim-up bar? A private beach? A stadium-style private theater in the basement?

SPEAK YOUR LOVE LANGUAGE

Hold hands as you walk around shopping for the exciting new décor. Surprise each other with gifts for the "new" space that you know your partner will love.

MAKE THE MOST OF IT

Perhaps this can be the start of an exciting rehab of your home(s). If you live separately, take turns collaborating on one room in each of your spaces. This kind of service builds trust and intimacy.

21 FIND YOUR FAMILY TREE

Where are your ancestors from? It's a question that many people ask at some point in their lives. Why not turn it into a date? On this date, you will not only learn more about your own DNA but you may also discover if you and your partner can trace your genealogies to similar parts of the world.

TIPS

- Set up an account on a genealogy website and see who you can track down in your extended family from archives. Make it into a guessing game! Write down your predictions of each other's genealogy and see who comes the closest.
- Call your parents, grandparents, or any other living relatives and ask them to tell stories about your family and what it was like for them growing up.

TALK ABOUT IT

Ask each other which era in history you would have most liked and least liked to have lived in. If you could take a time machine back to talk to any of your ancestors, who would it be and what would you ask them?

SPEAK YOUR LOVE LANGUAGE

Show an interest in understanding your partner's heritage by learning to cook a traditional dish from it. You could also find an appropriate restaurant and make a night out of appreciating your partner's roots. Learn how to say "I like you" or "I love you" in a language from your partner's heritage.

MAKE THE MOST OF IT

Order two DNA ancestry kits that you can complete and send back together to analyze your DNA. When you get your results, start filling in your family trees online and ask family members to add to them. See how far back in time you can trace your heritage.

22 COUPLE'S VISION BOARD

Why just focus on the present moment when you can make a date out of the future? Together, you will talk about and define your goals and dreams as a couple and explore how to make them a reality.

TIPS

- Make a list of all the categories of things that are important in your lives, such as family, finances, vacations, and retirement. List as many categories as you want.
- Search for and print out images representing these categories or cut them out of magazines. Attach them to a big poster or corkboard. Make sure they represent your dreams.
- When you are finished, hang your vision board in a prominent area of your home(s) so that you can see it every day.

TALK ABOUT IT

In order for this date to make an impact, you will have to have a lot of conversations about your goals and dreams. Dig deep to identify your goals and dreams and cocreate your vision of the future together.

SPEAK YOUR LOVE LANGUAGE

Talk about the gifts you would like to buy each other in the future or the kinds of romantic, sexy vacations you would like to take together. Be sure to add positive and inspiring words about each other to your vision board.

MAKE THE MOST OF IT

Instead of cutting out generic photos of the type of house you want in the future, why not find an actual house that you could see yourself living in and take selfies in front of it for your vision board? This process can be repeated for any other category of goal.

SUPER DATE
PASSIONATE PORTRAITS

Posing naked for your partner can be a very erotic experience or a nerve-racking one, depending on how you feel in your skin. This date is for couples who want to be daring and push each other outside of their comfort zones. You'll pose completely naked and sketch, draw, or paint each other on paper or canvas.

TIPS

- You make up the rules of your art session. Would you prefer to have a sheet artfully draped over parts of your body for comfort? Would you like all the lights on to be sure your partner can see every square inch? Do what makes both of you feel comfortable and empowered in your bodies.
- Drawing and painting aren't the only options for this art project. With each other's consent, you could pose for photos instead. You can keep the photos or delete them right after feeling the thrill of posing nude for each other.
- Maybe you'd both like to have frame-worthy artistic nudes of each other created. Commission custom nude portraits from an artist, or book a photo session for nudes with a photographer. With a little research you'll find an artist or photographer with a style that suits your needs.

TALK ABOUT IT

Ask your partner what they are thinking and feeling as they pose naked for you. Tell them how beautiful they are and how turned on you are. What sexual favors would you like to trade when this art session is over?

SPEAK YOUR LOVE LANGUAGE

Being naked is a vulnerable state for many people. Check in with your partner and reassure them if they're feeling nervous or overly self-critical. Touch and caress your partner and tell

them all about your favorite parts of their body. Splurge on a bottle of wine to help each other get into the mood of the date, or surprise your partner with a gift of a silky robe to slip into when the art session is over.

MAKE THE MOST OF IT

When you're finished painting on canvas, why not try a little body painting? Spread out an old sheet, lay down, close your eyes, and let your partner paint your body. The feeling of the cold paint and the paintbrush bristles on your skin can heighten your senses. You can take turns painting each other's bodies and see where your creativity takes you. Use water-based paints and they'll wash right off in the shower.

FUN & GAMES

One of the greatest gifts you can give in a relationship is the freedom to laugh and be playful. It's important to have balance in life, and that includes time to have fun and play games.

The bucket list dates in this chapter are all about playfulness and the competitive spirit we find when playing together. Remember when you were a kid and you played games with your friends? Those times were probably when you felt the most alive, right? That all shouldn't end just because you are an adult now.

In my personal experience, a sense of humor and a willingness to play are two of the most significant and satisfying things to have in a relationship. Playfulness simply feels good; it makes us laugh. It also supports relationships in a variety of ways. Something as simple as a playful remark or gesture can loosen up a tense situation, reminding you that whatever stresses you're under, you're still in a safe and loving relationship.

Games can also foster a sense of competition. While it's fun to try to win, don't forget that winning isn't everything. Even if you're a highly competitive person, keep in mind that, ultimately, you're on a team with your partner. Remember, you want your play to strengthen your bond!

With the right attitude, playing together can increase communication and satisfaction in your relationship. If life gets you into a rut, play can serve to resurrect the positive, giddy aspects of your partnership. Having fun together promotes intimacy and joy.

Bottom line: Playful couples are happy couples. Get ready to have some fun!

NEVER HAVE I EVER

Traditionally a drinking game, in Never Have I Ever you and your partner take turns sharing things you have never done. If your partner has done one of the things that you've never done, they take a drink (and vice versa). The game typically goes round and round with no defined end, but you can also play up to a certain number of points and declare a winner. This is a great way to get to know secrets about each other!

TIPS

- Instead of playing this as a drinking game, you can keep track of points: Start the game holding up all 10 of your fingers, and put a finger down each time you've done one of the things your partner says they haven't done before. The first person with all 10 fingers down loses.
- Make this a sexy game! You can take turns sharing places you've never had sex or sexual positions you've never tried.

TALK ABOUT IT

You're bound to learn something new about your partner by playing this game, so take the opportunity to ask them to tell you more about the things they have or haven't done before. If you learn that your partner hasn't tried a sexual position that you have, ask them if they'd like to give it a try tonight!

SPEAK YOUR LOVE LANGUAGE

Buy a special bottle of wine or mix your partner's favorite drink before starting the game. During the game, tell your partner what you love learning about them, and be honest if anything you've learned is a turn-on.

MAKE THE MOST OF IT

Brainstorm thematic topics, such as pranks and misadventures, quintessential movies and TV shows, or sexual exploits so that you can play a few rounds of the game.

25 JUMPING FOR JOY

You may have played on a trampoline before, whether it was in gym class, your backyard growing up, or maybe a neighbor's backyard. But have you experienced trampolines as an adult? This is the perfect time to bring back your inner child and have some fun jumping around with your partner at a trampoline park.

TIPS

- Play a game of dodgeball with your partner while you are jumping in the trampoline park.
- Many venues offer the opportunity to joust while jumping, so try that with your partner as well.
- Challenge each other to a game of trampoline basketball. You can both pretend you're Michael Jordan and go up for a slam dunk!

TALK ABOUT IT

Talk about childhood memories around playtime, games, and activities. What were your favorite games to play? What did you not like to play and why? A fun and silly trampoline date is the perfect time to share some childhood stories.

SPEAK YOUR LOVE LANGUAGE

Even though you are going to be bouncing around, you can still touch each other and hold hands while you do it. Help each other with your words, and compliment your partner on a cool move they pulled off.

MAKE THE MOST OF IT

Trampoline parks are popular destinations and can get crowded; however, some also offer private rentals. If you don't want to be in a crowded space with strangers, consider a more intimate private rental so that you can have a space all to yourselves.

26 THE GREAT ESCAPE ROOM

An escape room is an immersive game where you and your partner (and more people if you want to invite others) work cooperatively to discover clues, solve puzzles and riddles, and complete tasks in order to "escape" a room. You typically have a limited amount of time to figure out how to escape in order to win the game.

TIPS

- Escape room venues usually have many rooms with different levels of difficulty. Choose the level you think will be most comfortable for the two of you.
- Have a private "competition" between you and your partner. Whoever figures out the least clues has to take the "winner" out for dinner.

TALK ABOUT IT

Being trapped anywhere can bring up thoughts of claustrophobia, the fear of small, enclosed spaces. Are you or your partner claustrophobic? Do either of you have any phobias that you are hoping to overcome?

SPEAK YOUR LOVE LANGUAGE

Tease and touch each other as you are looking for clues and trying to find a way to escape. When your partner figures out one of the steps toward escaping, tell them how proud you are of them.

MAKE THE MOST OF IT

After the escape room, you can get creative and make a scavenger hunt at home. Each of you can create a series of clues for your partner, then time each other as you race to solve them. The person who completes their scavenger hunt first can decide what their prize will be from the loser.

27 LASER TAG LOVE AFFAIR

Laser tag is a classic, high-energy game of tag played with pretend guns that fire infrared beams. Each player wears an infrared-sensitive target on their chest, and you aim to shoot other people's targets to eliminate them from the game.

TIPS

- If one of you has played but the other hasn't, guide and coach your partner before and during the game. If you're playing a non-private game with other players, arrange to be on the same side so that you can play cooperatively.
- If you're both pros, play on opposite teams and create challenges for each other, like firing with only one arm.

TALK ABOUT IT

Talk about the merits of teamwork or some of its difficulties. Do you like working in a team or alone? Why? If you were, did you like being on each other's team?

SPEAK YOUR LOVE LANGUAGE

Help each other put on your laser tag gear. If you are on the same team, try to perform acts of service by supporting each other in the game. You can also hold hands to lead your partner to a good hiding spot or crouch together to sneak up on an opponent.

MAKE THE MOST OF IT

Find a large activity center that has laser tag and a lot of other fun things to do. Many of these kinds of venues also have bowling alleys, go-karts, miniature golf, bouncy slides, and other similar activities. Make your date into an evening or a whole day of fun!

28 DISC DATING

Disc golf, sometimes known as "frolf" or "folf," is a flying disc sport with rules similar to golf. Just like golf, you throw your disc as many times as it takes to get it into a target (usually a basket), then continue on for 9 or 18 "holes." The goal is to have the lowest total number of throws at each hole.

TIPS

- Add some affectionate or sexy incentives to the game. At each hole, the winner can ask for a hug, kiss, neck massage, or anything else they want.
- Add challenges to the game. At each hole, the winner can give the loser a task to perform, like sit-ups, push-ups, or anything else they feel like.
- If you can't find a disc golf course near you (or if you just want a do-it-yourself experience), set up your own course in your backyard or a nearby park.

TALK ABOUT IT

Create a new topic of conversation at each hole. For example, you could name three things you like about your partner's body, three things you like about their personality, or three things they don't know about you yet. Get creative at each hole!

SPEAK YOUR LOVE LANGUAGE

Compliment your partner on their play technique. The game can still be competitive with mutual encouragement. Perform acts of service for your partner, like carrying their equipment from one hole to the next.

MAKE THE MOST OF IT

Pack a picnic to enjoy after you complete a game of disc golf. Make your favorite foods and bring your favorite drinks. Add some flameless candles to set a romantic mood.

BUBBLE FLING

Many people have never heard the word "zorbing," but chances are they'd recognize it if they saw it. Zorbing is rolling inside a giant inflatable ball (usually made of transparent plastic) down a gentle slope or on a level surface. It's like being inside a big globe.

TIPS

- You might not want to eat or drink too much before you go zorbing just in case your stomach can't handle the excitement!
- Incentivize your play with bets on who will last the longest or travel the farthest in the orb before getting tired.
- Choose a venue where zorbing is combined with water play for an experience akin to being at a waterpark in an orb.

TALK ABOUT IT

Since you've now experienced being enclosed in a bubble, talk about what it would be like to live in a glass dome on another planet. Would you volunteer to live in a space colony? Why or why not?

SPEAK YOUR LOVE LANGUAGE

Shout encouraging words to your partner; it takes some courage to do this activity. Hug each other and hold hands when you get out of your orbs to express your love and affection.

MAKE THE MOST OF IT

You may need to travel to find a zorbing location, which makes it even more important to get the most out of your zorbing trip. Turn this date into a daylong event! Choose a few other activities to do after you go zorbing, such as bowling, roller-skating or hiking. Top off the day with a romantic dinner in the evening.

30 BULL'S-EYE!

Archery has been around for millennia, and axe throwing has its roots in the logging competitions of yesteryear. But what is old is new again, as both have experienced a resurgence in popularity. For this date, you'll be brushing up on your target practice skills.

TIPS

- Whether you decide to shoot or throw, find a venue with instructors on hand to teach you and your partner how to handle a bow and arrow or an axe safely.
- Many axe-throwing venues have a bar atmosphere. Try a place where you can combine axe throwing with food and drink to make for a well-rounded date.
- Invite another couple to turn this into a double date (or invite a group of friends). It's always fun to have other people to compete with.

TALK ABOUT IT

Ask each other if you've ever handled a weapon before. How did it make you feel? Which weapon would you least want to be the victim of? While it might sound like a morbid conversation, it can be very interesting to see if your partner has different thoughts on these topics than you do.

SPEAK YOUR LOVE LANGUAGE

Accurately shooting an arrow or throwing an axe is harder than it looks. Help each other and offer words of encouragement. If souvenirs are available, buy one for your partner.

MAKE THE MOST OF IT

Instead of choosing either archery or axe throwing, why not do both? You could start out early in the day at one location for archery, then meet up with friends in the evening at another location for axe throwing over drinks and dinner. You could even add a trip to a shooting range in between!

31 DATING, UNSCRIPTED

Improv is a fun way to challenge yourself to be spontaneous and creative. If you're not familiar with improvisation, it's a form of theater (most often comedic) where the performance is unplanned and unscripted; actors riff off one another and the audience. Take a class together on this date.

TIPS

- Remember: In improv, there are no right or wrong lines, but there are some rules to help drive the performance forward. Always answer "yes." Denying or negating anything in a scene often brings it to an immediate halt.
- Just keep going. It doesn't matter if a scene doesn't make a lot of sense: Continue making statements, developing a story, and agreeing with everything.
- Improv is an art, not a science. You don't have to be funny to have a successful scene, but you do have to commit.

TALK ABOUT IT

In improv, we basically make up stories. So, ask each other what your favorite books and stories have been throughout your lives. Why did you like them the best? If either of you were in a play or musical earlier in life, talk about those experiences, too.

SPEAK YOUR LOVE LANGUAGE

Since improv taps into your silly and playful side, buy your partner a gag gift to go along with your date. Performing can be nerve-racking for some people, so be sure to encourage and support each other before, during, and after the class.

MAKE THE MOST OF IT

Keep it going! When your improv class is over, remember the characters you've created, take them home (or wherever else you want), and put them in a new scene.

32 MIXOLOGIST ROULETTE

In order to play drinking roulette, you need a roulette wheel and a number of shot glasses to arrange around it (it's up to you how many). Each of the glasses should be filled with a beverage and labeled with a number that corresponds to a number on the wheel. To play, just spin the wheel; whatever number it lands on is the glass that you must down.

TIPS

- You can play the game with alcohol or a nonalcoholic beverage of your choice. If using alcohol, you might not want to fill the shot glasses to the brim so that you don't get too drunk too fast.
- Each of you should fill half of the glasses so that neither of you knows what's in every glass before you drink.
- Try getting a little wild by combining several drinks so that you're surprised with a new taste every shot!

TALK ABOUT IT

Talk about parties you've attended. Did you play drinking games at those parties, or did you avoid them (and why)? For a deeper conversation, talk about luck and chance. When have you felt like you've really lucked out?

SPEAK YOUR LOVE LANGUAGE

Use words of encouragement when your partner "loses" and has to drink a shot. Prepare dinner or buy takeout beforehand so that no one is drinking on an empty stomach. Surprise your partner with a bottle of their favorite drink afterward as a gift.

MAKE THE MOST OF IT

Instead of limiting yourselves to roulette, you could create your own Las Vegas night by adding blackjack, poker, rummy, or even bingo. If you feel like spicing things up, play a game of strip poker.

33 WIND TUNNEL OF LOVE

For those of us who are too afraid to do the real thing, indoor skydiving is the perfect alternative. It takes place inside an enclosed wind tunnel with controlled air blowing upward. An instructor will help you lean into the wind, and then you'll be floating. No jumping out of a plane or free-falling!

TIPS

- You can dive one at a time or together. Doing it together is more fun and brings you closer to your partner.
- If you choose to dive together, try to do some of the tricks and formations that real skydivers do.

TALK ABOUT IT

Have a conversation about your fears and how much money it would take to get you to face them. For example, if you fear real skydiving, is there any amount of money someone could pay you to make you do it? See if you both have limits.

SPEAK YOUR LOVE LANGUAGE

Even if you're not free-falling out of a plane, this activity can still be scary for some people. Be encouraging with your words, hold hands before and during the experience, and commemorate the date by purchasing photos at the end of your session.

MAKE THE MOST OF IT

If this is your first time indoor skydiving, you'll need to learn how to maintain a stable flying position. This can be fun to do as a couple. To make the most of this experience, book an additional time slot to learn how to move your bodies in the tunnel together. Challenge yourselves by asking your instructor to teach you a new move, such as how to turn, move forward or backward, slide side to side, or go up and down.

RIDE THE WAVES

Turn this bucket list date into a bucket list trip! Visit a tropical destination where you can participate in fun activities like surfing and parasailing. Surfing is a rush once you've established balance on your board; parasailing is thrilling when you take off, then feels quite relaxing once you're soaring.

TIPS

- If this is your first time surfing, find a resort that offers surfing lessons or a surf camp. It takes practice to learn how to surf, so it's best to have access to daily lessons and reps.
- When you go parasailing, you may want to find a venue that allows the two of you to go out at the same time.
- When planning your bucket list trip, choose a destination that offers a wide variety of fun activities in addition to surfing and parasailing, such as riding Jet Skis and sailing.

TALK ABOUT IT

Since the focus of this bucket list trip is fun and games in the water, talk about what other water activities you would like to add to your bucket list. Some ideas include going on a windjammer cruise, buying a sailboat, or trying recreational diving.

SPEAK YOUR LOVE LANGUAGE

Surfing and parasailing can be challenging and exhilarating! Hold hands while you are parasailing, and offer lots of encouragement to each other while you are learning to surf. Learning to surf will take the most trial and error, so keep your eyes peeled for any acts of service you can perform to help each other stay positive. Buy a photo package when you go parasailing.

MAKE THE MOST OF IT

Make sure that you choose a venue with many water sports
options. Get as extreme as you can tolerate. Maybe you'll want
to experience flyboarding above the water, cliff jumping, or
whitewater rafting.

5

HOMEGROWN DATES

This chapter is all about DIY (do-it-yourself) dates that you can go on in and around your home(s). These are low-risk, budget-conscious ideas that are still fun and different. Just because you are at home doesn't mean you have to do the same old, same old daily routine.

Too often, couples get stuck in the daily grind—in life and at home. We get up in the morning, go to work, come home, cook dinner, care for our kids and/or pets (if you have either or both), and repeat the next day.

I know how it can be. There was a time when I had little money, and there was also a time when I had little children. Sometimes, I just wanted to stay at home and have a "homegrown" date! Dates at home are so important, especially when you may not have the resources or time you need to go out and explore the world. Thankfully, you *can* shake things up and make being at home into an exciting date.

The key to these dates is to try to forget that you're at home. Homegrown dates are designed for you to pretend that you're in another world, even if you haven't stepped foot outside your home. All it takes is a little imagination on your part.

Try to get rid of distractions. Turn off your phones and the TV. Don't let everyday details get in the way of you having a romantic and exciting date.

Homegrown dates are a beautiful opportunity to redefine what your home means to you and how you connect with your partner in such a familiar place. You can make your home more than just where you live—you can transform it into a place of romance.

35 THE QUESTION GAME

When life gets in the way, we can forget to think deeply about our lives. Too often, our conversations as couples turn into little more than "What happened at work today?" So, this homegrown date gives you the opportunity to dig deep, learn more about each other, and have a little fun while you do it!

TIPS

- Get a book to help guide your conversations, such as *The Book of Questions* by Gregory Stock, or write down your own questions to ask each other. Come up with at least 10 each because you will need enough questions to last you all night.
- Let the questions guide you into other related questions. Don't just settle for "yes" or "no" answers. Probe deeper and ask a lot of follow-up questions.

TALK ABOUT IT

This homegrown date is *all* about talking! That's the point—to talk about crazy concepts that most people don't even think about their whole lives. So, after you are done with your questions, wrap up your date by talking about why you think most people don't think about deep topics like these.

SPEAK YOUR LOVE LANGUAGE

While you ask each other questions, snuggle up in a blanket on the couch or in front of a fire. In between questions, tell each other at least one thing that you love about each other.

MAKE THE MOST OF IT

Make it into a game! Instead of just asking your partner a question, try to predict what they are going to say. And if you are right, you get a point. If you're not, they get a point. Add up the points to see who won. Then the loser has to do something really romantic for the winner.

36 THE PERFECT PLAYLIST

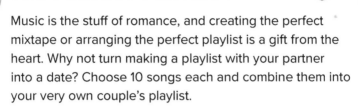

Music is the stuff of romance, and creating the perfect mixtape or arranging the perfect playlist is a gift from the heart. Why not turn making a playlist with your partner into a date? Choose 10 songs each and combine them into your very own couple's playlist.

TIPS

- Make a romantic playlist of songs that you can play when you both feel like getting sexy and having some intimate time alone.
- Make a party playlist of fun, upbeat songs that you can play when you are in the mood to crank it up.
- Make an autobiographical playlist with the most meaningful and memorable songs from your lives.

TALK ABOUT IT

With each song you choose, talk about why you chose it. What about the song speaks to you? It is the lyrics? The tune? The beat? Does it remind you of a special (or difficult) time in your life? Did you see a live performance of it?

SPEAK YOUR LOVE LANGUAGE

Don't forget to choose songs that remind you of each other. When you play them, tell your partner what about these songs makes you think of them and why you like, love, or care for them so much.

MAKE THE MOST OF IT

Don't just make this playlist and forget about it. Put it on your phones and play it in the car, at home, or for your kids. You may want to keep adding to it as the years go by because there is always new music that will speak to your soul.

37 BUILD A BUCKET LIST

Even though this book is a bucket list for dating, that doesn't mean you can't make a different kind of bucket list while you're reading it! On this date, you'll ask yourselves a classic question: What do you and your partner want to do before you die? This gives you the opportunity to get creative and dream big together to make the most of this life while you're still here.

TIPS

- Make your lists independently at first, writing down as many ideas as you possibly can. Then come back together and compare your ideas.
- Compile a master list from both of your individual lists, then go through it and cross out the things that you or your partner absolutely will *not* do.

TALK ABOUT IT

Review your bucket lists together and talk about them in detail. For example, if you want to go zip-lining, where do you want to do it? In your hometown? Or somewhere new and different, like a big cruise ship or Costa Rica? Describing the details and naming your preferences only make it more fun to dream about the possibilities.

SPEAK YOUR LOVE LANGUAGE

Talk about your "bucket list" ways to receive love. Ask your partner what three things would make them feel the most loved by you, then do those things for them (on this date or later if you can't make them happen that night).

MAKE THE MOST OF IT

Don't stop at dreaming! Set some plans in motion. Rank all of the items on your bucket list in order of importance (the ones you want to do first being the most important). Then, take the top five, pull out a calendar, and make definite plans.

38 LIVING ROOM PICNIC

Yes, you make dinner at home all the time, but how often do you have a *picnic* at home? You don't even need to go anywhere for this date, and yet it's still different from just having dinner at home . . . because you're not eating at the table—you're on a picnic!

TIPS

- You can have a living room picnic, a backyard picnic, or even a bed picnic. Just grab a blanket and spread it out. Then, get a picnic basket and fill it with whatever you like: finger sandwiches; a platter of meats, cheeses, and olives; a fruit salad; and/or some wine.
- Wait until it's dark and light some candles to set a romantic mood.
- Research and experiment with new cocktail recipes to mix during your romantic picnic.

TALK ABOUT IT

You could share childhood memories of a school picnic or a family get-together. Did you play any games that were particularly fun for you? Why not try those games again?

SPEAK YOUR LOVE LANGUAGE

Going on a picnic in your own home lends itself to touching, hand-holding, and heads placed in laps. Buy each other little romantic presents ahead of time to make the night special.

MAKE THE MOST OF IT

Don't just make regular picnic food for this date. Get creative! Before the date, try to find some gourmet foods that you don't get to have every day. Level up from a ho-hum peanut butter and jelly sandwich to fig jam, aged cheese, and rosemary crackers. It's romantic, special, and fun!

39   DIARY DATING

By journaling together, you and your partner can both reflect upon your lives, memories, dreams, and goals. On the evening of this date, you could have some of the most intimate conversations you've ever had as a couple, deepening your trust and intimacy. Put away your phones, turn off the TV, and be present with each other as you journal.

TIPS

- Pick a few writing prompts that you'd like to work on together. Prompts could include writing about a favorite childhood memory, listing five goals you'd like to achieve in the next five years, or describing your proudest achievement.
- Find a comfortable place to sit and write together. Set a timer for 10 minutes and write about the same prompt.
- Share your writing with each other. If you feel uncomfortable sharing, talk about that discomfort.

TALK ABOUT IT

Ask your partner about their writing. Be curious and attentive to each other. If a difficult subject is raised, be honest about what you have difficulty verbalizing.

SPEAK YOUR LOVE LANGUAGE

Opening up to each other can leave you both feeling vulnerable. Be tender with each other. Cuddle up on the couch while you talk. Or sit on the floor, holding hands, and look into your partner's eyes while they speak.

MAKE THE MOST OF IT

Turn the focus of your writing prompts to your relationship. What three things do you admire most in your partner? What can you do to be more supportive of your partner? List three compliments you want to pay your partner.

MEDITATE TOGETHER

I know a lot of people think meditation is a little "woo-woo," but not only is it very relaxing—it is also great for your health! We all have busy lives; taking some time to learn to meditate together can really calm your minds and create a deeper bond between you and your partner.

TIPS

- If you have room in your home(s), create a space just for meditation. Make sure it's quiet and peaceful.
- Listen to soothing meditation music that you both enjoy while you meditate. Or, if you need help with the process, choose a guided meditation to listen to together.
- Make sure your room is dark, and turn on some mood lighting, such as a lava lamp or dim Christmas lights.

TALK ABOUT IT

After you meditate, talk about your experiences. Did you like it? Do you feel more relaxed? Did you get bored? How can you both get more out of the experience the next time you meditate?

SPEAK YOUR LOVE LANGUAGE

Sit or lie next to each other so that you can hold hands while you meditate. Send each other loving thoughts while meditating, and tell your partner how much you appreciate them.

MAKE THE MOST OF IT

Meditation is a great way to focus on your goals and dreams because it allows you to access your subconscious mind. Before you meditate, talk with your partner about what you want to focus on. Then, while you meditate, try to visualize what you want your future to look like. This will program your subconscious mind to work toward making your visualization a reality.

41 FINE DINING AND DATING

Whether or not you like to cook, everyone likes to eat, right? Well, this date is more than just cooking boxed mac and cheese for dinner. Instead, you and your partner will find a *new* gourmet meal that you can make together. Never fear: Not only will it be delicious, but it will be fun, too.

TIPS

- Make grocery shopping part of the date experience. (If you can't, one or both of you can get ingredients ahead of time.)
- Try a new wine or beer pairing to go along with the dish you are preparing.
- "Style" or plate your food like a professional chef. Make sure to take pictures!

TALK ABOUT IT

Talk about your likes and dislikes when it comes to food. You probably already know many of them, so get creative; for example, ask your partner: "If you had to eat only one thing for the rest of your life, what would it be?" or "What's the strangest food combination you've ever tried?"

SPEAK YOUR LOVE LANGUAGE

Feed each other as you are making the meal. Put your arms around your partner or pinch them on the backside to be flirty and playful.

MAKE THE MOST OF IT

Create a fine dining experience at home! Break out the good china, cloth napkins, and candles for ambience, and prepare a multi-course experience with an appetizer to start the meal and a dessert to end it. If this feels like an overwhelming amount of cooking all at once, you can each prepare either an appetizer or a dessert ahead of time to reheat and serve with the meal you cook together.

42

HOMEGROWN DANCE CHALLENGE

Learning a choreographed dance routine with your partner takes teamwork, patience, perseverance . . . and an Internet connection. You can find tutorials online covering everything from the latest social media dance challenge to the steps of a classic ballroom dance.

TIPS

- Brainstorm what you'd like your dance routine to be. You can search by song title, dance name, or social media hashtag (if you're looking for the latest craze).
- Keep your body loose and the mood light and have fun with the dance! There's no grade, no audience, and no pressure.
- It might take a few tries to get the moves right, so be patient and encourage each other.

TALK ABOUT IT

Do you enjoy performing in front of others? Or do you have performance anxiety? Talk about a memorable performance you once had and how you felt after it was over.

SPEAK YOUR LOVE LANGUAGE

Hold hands, embrace, and dip your partner. Depending on the dance, there can be lots of opportunities to touch each other on this date. Tell your partner you like the way they move their body, and give each other compliments for mastering these smooth moves.

MAKE THE MOST OF IT

Take your dance routine to the next level and let the world see it. Post it on your social media outlet of choice, use hashtags to make your video searchable, and claim your bragging rights as a couple for learning the routine and putting it out there for everyone to see.

43 BE MY BARTENDER

Be each other's bartender for a night at home. Concoct your own made-up cocktails from scratch!

TIPS

- Talk about which liquors you like and don't like. Buy a few small bottles of the ones you both like. Figure out what kinds of mixers you enjoy. Do you like sweet flavors? Sour? Salty?
- Start experimenting with as many different combinations as you can, and come up with a new cocktail to name together and make again in the future.
- Keep each drink small. You don't want to get too drunk, and you won't waste very much liquid if you don't like a particular concoction.

TALK ABOUT IT

As you go through each new cocktail, talk in detail about what you like or don't like about it. What do you think could make it better? Ask your partner for their opinions, then take their advice on how to improve upon each one.

SPEAK YOUR LOVE LANGUAGE

Remember to flirt! After all, you're sitting at a bar with an attractive bartender serving you delicious cocktails. It's meant to be fun and carefree, so compliment each other and get closer. Feel free to get touchy-feely on this date.

MAKE THE MOST OF IT

Add more technique to your mixology date. Pick up fruits and herbs you think would pair well and try muddling them into your concoctions. Or, if you have a blender, perhaps some of these cocktails could be blended with ice. Have a blind taste test and see if you can tell what your partner put in a particular drink (and vice versa).

44 THE GREAT COUPLE'S BAKE-OFF

This date is a competition between the two of you to see who can make the best bakery item. From savory to sweet, baked goods come in all flavors. So whether you have a sweet tooth or not, this bake-off will be both fun and filling!

TIPS

- Choose a baked good—like croissants or cream puffs—and see who can make the best version.
- You can try choosing a dessert that brings back warm childhood memories to introduce your partner to a longtime favorite.
- Enlist a friend or family member after your date to judge whose masterpiece is the best.

TALK ABOUT IT

What is the most delicious dessert you have ever had? Why do you like it so much? As you bake, you can also talk about how you might create an entirely new recipe that the two of you can call your own.

SPEAK YOUR LOVE LANGUAGE

Get yourselves gifts, such as a chef's hat or an apron, to commemorate your bake-off. Or, you can get a little silly and flirty by having a small "food fight" in the kitchen. Perform an act of service for your partner by doing all the cleanup afterward.

MAKE THE MOST OF IT

Step up your baking game and challenge each other by selecting a more daring dessert. Instead of chocolate chip cookies, how about crème brûlée? Depending on what you select, you may need to invest in some extra equipment (like a butane crème brûlée torch), so be sure to prepare your tools in advance.

45 HOMEBREWING AND WINEMAKING FOR TWO

It's way too easy to just go to your local liquor store and buy a bottle of wine or some beer. But that's not too exciting, so this date involves trying to make your own wine or beer at home. It's fun to pretend that you have a new career as a winemaker or brewer. And in the end, you'll have a new wine or beer to sample. What can beat that?

TIPS

- You'll need to purchase either a brewing or winemaking kit. A proper kit will provide everything you need to make a batch of the drink of your choice.
- Both brewing and winemaking require a fermentation period that can last days to weeks depending on what you make. You might want to make your beer or wine in the garage if you can, just in case you find the fermentation smell too off-putting.

TALK ABOUT IT

Talk about the first time you ever tasted alcohol. Did you like it? Why did you try it? Did you sneak it at a party as a teenager? Did your parents know that you were drinking?

SPEAK YOUR LOVE LANGUAGE

Homebrewing and winemaking take time so order takeout for you and your partner to keep your energy up. Surprise your partner with a little romantic gift, such as their favorite wine or beer to drink during the date, since you'll be waiting a while before you can sample your DIY concoctions.

MAKE THE MOST OF IT

Plan a follow-up date for when the wine or beer is ready for tasting. You can go out for dinner and have a nightcap at home or make dinner to pair with your beer or wine.

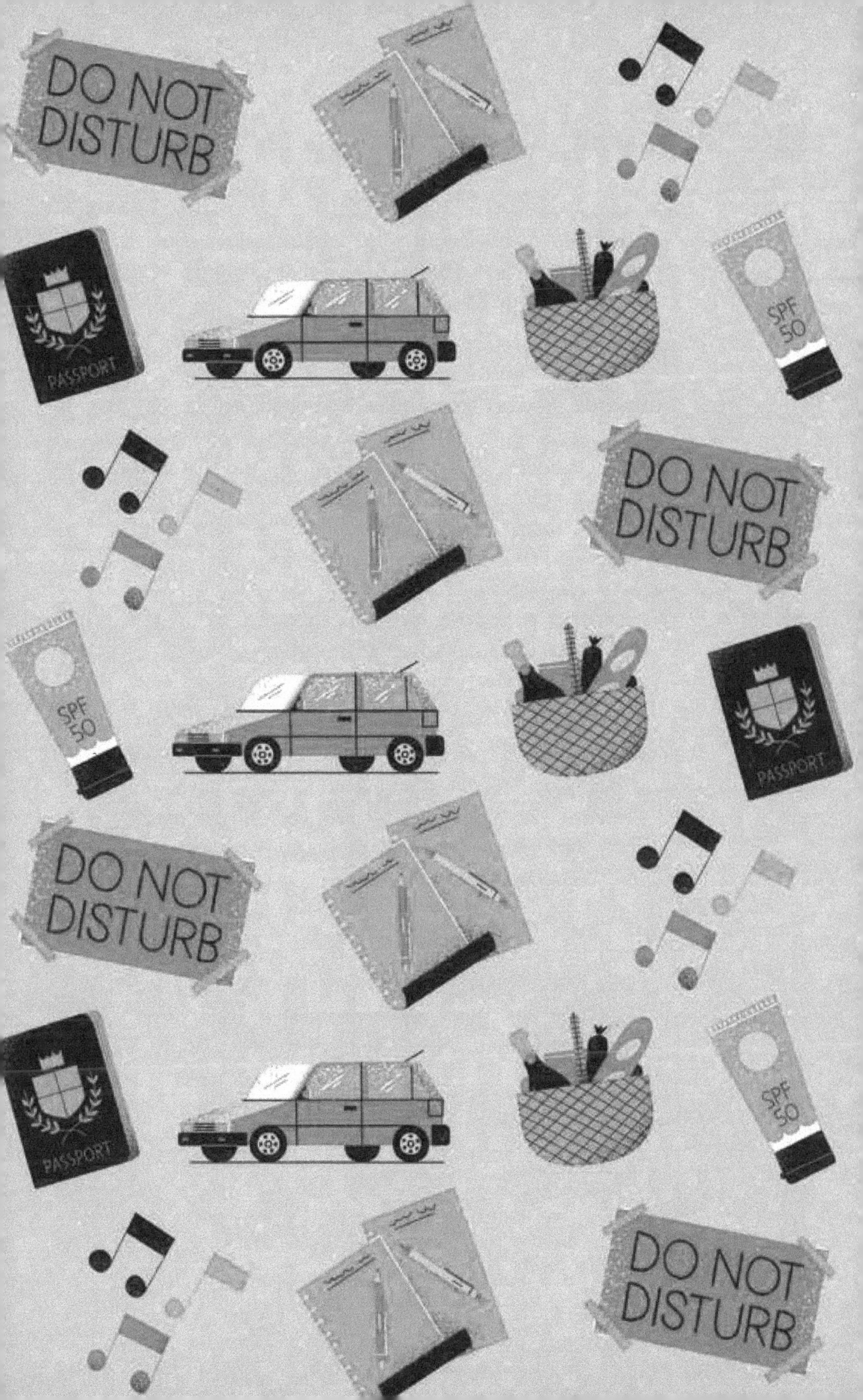
DO NOT DISTURB
PASSPORT
SPF 50

SUPER DATE
PAMPER YOUR PARTNER

Manicures and pedicures are a great way to spoil yourself and your partner. You can incorporate polish or just focus on a nice exfoliation and cuticle and nail trim. It's fun to pamper each other with massage oils and lotions, too.

TIPS

- Collect all the necessary equipment ahead of time. You'll need a basin and bowl for soaking your feet and hands, nail clippers, a cuticle pusher, nail files, lotion, a pumice stone, and nail polish.
- You can invest in a foot spa to soak your feet in. The bubbles and heat are soothing and relaxing and soften the skin on your feet.
- Give each other foot and/or hand massages as part of the date. They are sensuous and just feel really good!

TALK ABOUT IT

Since manicures and pedicures are relaxing, talk about your favorite ways to get away from the stress of life. Maybe you take time to relax regularly, and maybe you don't. Regardless, tell each other what you love about relaxing and make a plan for how to do it more often.

SPEAK YOUR LOVE LANGUAGE

This date naturally lends itself to touching through massage and hand-holding. Don't forget to compliment your partner. You can also buy them a small "spa gift" to remember your date.

MAKE THE MOST OF IT

If you're using nail polish, get creative with designs or add a stencil to your supplies purchase. Remember, it doesn't have to look perfect! Also, you don't have to stop at the manicure and pedicure. Why not have a full "spa evening" and give each other full body massages?

6

SEX & INTIMACY

What would a book on bucket list dating be without a chapter on sex and intimacy? After all, that's a big part of what romance is, isn't it?

Sex is naturally exciting and exhilarating in the beginning of a relationship. But over time it may become more routine and boring and might happen less or stop altogether. Regardless of where you are in your sexual journey with each other, you don't have to settle for a ho-hum existence when it comes to intimacy. You can always revive it! And it can be better than ever if you put in the effort.

It is a fact that sex creates stronger bonds between people. The chemicals that are released during intercourse generate a strong emotional connection between partners. Sex also creates and strengthens trust. You can even discover new things about each other through sex.

I know from experience how sex can make or break a relationship. Without it, sometimes couples just can't seem to stay close, and partners can grow resentful of each other as time goes on. Even if you're still having sex but it becomes boring, things won't be as good as they could be if you spiced things up!

Paramount in any discussion of physical intimacy is consent. It's important that you talk to your partner about what they will and will not do. Placing your trust in each other means never breaking that consent. Just as simply as it's given, it can be taken away, so communicate before, during, and after sex. You can establish a safe word with each other that immediately pulls the plug on any sexual scenario. Remember to go slow with each other. There's no rush! And you should only explore things you're both comfortable with.

LEAVE THE WINDOWS OPEN

This date is a great way to be "bad" while staying safe. Plus, you'll be bad together, so you'll get to share a mutual feeling of getting away with something exciting.

Have sex at home with the windows open, but keep the blinds closed. The fresh air will make you feel like you're outside, and the thrill of wondering if anyone can hear you will be titillating.

TIPS

- Sex in public is a misdemeanor in many states, and any "lewd" act in public could be legally problematic. Stay safe inside your home without putting on a show that others could see.
- If you've always wanted to have sex in a car in a secluded place, create a pretend scenario inside your garage with the door shut.

TALK ABOUT IT

It's important to have a conversation before you get this date started. Are you comfortable with the idea that someone could hear you being intimate together? If not, then agree to skip this date. Does the idea of being heard turn you on? Tell your partner.

SPEAK YOUR LOVE LANGUAGE

Talk dirty to each other while you're having sex. Compliment your partner's body and tell them how much you want them. Be specific about what you like. Always remember to ask periodically if they are comfortable and to make sure they feel safe.

MAKE THE MOST OF IT

Want to feel even more like you're having sex outside? Play some ambient noise recordings.

48 FALLING FOR YOU

This date is more about emotional intimacy than sexual intimacy. In order to have the best possible romantic life, you need to stay connected to your partner emotionally. Take an evening to write each other romantic stories or letters about how you fell for each other.

TIPS

- Recount your first date and your first impressions of your partner. Then, write about some other special memories, such as the first time you had sex. It's illuminating to hear recollections of a memorable time you shared together from your partner's perspective.
- Set the mood for your letter-writing date with candlelight, drinks, and romantic music.
- Try to write things that your partner doesn't know about. Maybe you've had thoughts through the years that you've never shared with them.

TALK ABOUT IT

Talk about the concept of soul mates. Do you believe in soul mates? Do you think that the two of you are soul mates? Why or why not? Or are you "twin flames" or "mirror souls"—literally two halves of the same soul? Get into a deep discussion of spirituality, your connection to each other, and possibly love.

SPEAK YOUR LOVE LANGUAGE

This date is all about using your words to tell your partner how much they mean to you or how you fell for them. Remember to touch and hug each other while you do it.

MAKE THE MOST OF IT

Instead of writing your thoughts, you could record audio or video relationship confessionals for your partner.

49   COUPLE'S HOTLINE

Phone sex is something you can do either the night before a date or as an actual date itself. If you do it the night before a date, spend the entire evening on it to create anticipation for when you finally get to see each other. As a full date, phone sex is a flexible option because you can be anywhere in the world and still jump on the line.

TIPS

- Be specific about what you want to do to you partner: The more details, the better.
- Even though you can't see each other over the phone, dress the part anyway. Put on something that makes you feel sexy and attractive. Your partner will hear it in your voice.
- If one or both of you are uncomfortable, you can always make light of the moment and chuckle your way through it. It's still fun whether you take it seriously or joke around about it.

TALK ABOUT IT

Since phone sex is similar to porn, talk about what types of porn you like to watch (if any). What are your turn-ons and turn-offs? If you don't like porn, talk about what you don't like about it. If you do like porn, talk about whether or not you would like to watch it together.

SPEAK YOUR LOVE LANGUAGE

Complimenting your partner's body and/or anything else you like about them is a perfect way to elevate this date. Tell your partner why you're attracted to them. Surprise them with a gift of sexy lingerie to wear before your phone sex date.

MAKE THE MOST OF IT

Get creative and role-play a scene during your call. Assume different identities and create a story line for your characters.

50 CLOTHING-OPTIONAL GAMES

Games are always fun to play, and if you are strapped for money or alone time, you can turn any game into a date. But the difference here is that you have to play whatever game you choose naked!

TIPS

- Give the game extra stakes. Maybe the loser has to do whatever sex act the winner wants them to do (with their complete consent, of course).
- Sit close to each other so that you can touch, flirt, and tease your partner as you play the game.
- Add food play to the game. Every time one of you loses, you have to lick a dollop of whipped cream (or something else of your choice) off your partner. Pick any food you're curious to play with.

TALK ABOUT IT

Talk about the games that you have liked and disliked throughout your life. Why do you like or dislike them? Also, how competitive do you think you are? Do you need to win, or are you playing games just to have fun?

SPEAK YOUR LOVE LANGUAGE

Buy your partner a game as a gift ahead of time. Sit close together while you play so that you can touch, tickle, and kiss each other during the game, and, of course, compliment your partner's naked body.

MAKE THE MOST OF IT

Instead of playing a classic board game or card game, why not make up your own game? This can be very creative and fun, and you can do it as part of the date itself. Just remember to do it naked or incorporate stripping into your rules.

51 SUNRISE AND SUNSET MAKE-OUT SESH

Sunrises and sunsets are inherently romantic, so why not turn them into a steamy make-out date? Even though the sun rises and sets every day, sometimes we take it for granted. Don't let another sunrise or sunset pass without making it a romantic, sexy, hot date.

TIPS

- Carefully choose a spot that has a great view of the sunrise or sunset and is secluded enough to give you privacy for your make-out session.
- If you can find a spot with a grassy or comfortable patch to spread a blanket, have your date out in the open air.
- If the weather is not temperate or you'd feel more comfortable inside your car, find a secluded and scenic spot to park and act like teenagers while you watch the sun come up or go down.

TALK ABOUT IT

Since this date is all about the beautiful scenery (including the scenery of your partner's body), talk about what other sights you would like to see in the world.

SPEAK YOUR LOVE LANGUAGE

Make a picnic for your partner as a gift for the date. Cuddle on the blanket with your arms around each other as you watch the beauty in the sky.

MAKE THE MOST OF IT

Don't forget to take pictures and videos of the moment! Snap photos of each other and record the sunrise or sunset as it happens. How often do we take the time to record this spectacle? You'll be capturing beautiful memories of your sunset date.

52 GAMBLING LAID BARE

There has to be a reason why people turned poker into a strip game, right? Well, now it's time for you and your partner to try it yourselves. The objective is for both of you to lose enough that you eventually get naked.

TIPS

- Before you start the game, talk about what rules you will follow. What counts as "stripping"? Does taking off an earring count? Or a watch? Or taking your hair down? If so, the game will be extended even longer (which is good).
- Set the mood. Light some candles, drink some wine, and prepare a cozy space at the table to play poker.

TALK ABOUT IT

Since strip poker is also about betting, talk about whether or not you like to gamble. If you do, why do you like it? The thrill? Or the potential to make money? If you don't like to gamble, why not? What are some things you would bet on—or *never* bet on?

SPEAK YOUR LOVE LANGUAGE

As you both gradually strip away your clothes, tell your partner what you would like to do with them sexually when the game is over. Play footsie under the table. Tease your partner with innuendo. You might even want to buy each other special clothes and undergarments that look sexier than what you normally wear every day.

MAKE THE MOST OF IT

You could combine the stripping with a drinking game, too. For every article of clothing you remove, you also have to take a shot or a sip of a drink of your choosing. When the game is over, don't forget to top off the date with some sexy lovemaking!

SEXY ACCOUTREMENTS

It's normal for your sex life to fall into a bit of a routine after a while. It can be hard to be creative when it comes to spicing things up. So, why not try some sex toys to help you along? Researching what kinds of sex toys you might be interested in trying together (or alone) can be a sexy way to open up about how you want to change up your routine and have some extra fun.

TIPS

- Start slow and small. For example, try playing with food like hot fudge or whipped cream as a way to build up to toys.
- Choose toys that make you feel good! Not everyone is into sex toys that are wild and crazy.
- If you feel really adventurous, then go as far as you want into getting down and dirty. For some people, anything goes!

TALK ABOUT IT

Before you choose the sex toys you want to use, talk to your partner about your feelings and interests. You may have differing levels of adventurousness, so make sure you are on the same page. What are your limits? What are your must-haves?

SPEAK YOUR LOVE LANGUAGE

You can use some dirty, sexy talk when you are trying out your new toy collection. Remember to compliment your partner and touch them in a loving way, too.

MAKE THE MOST OF IT

If you really want to make things kinky, you can watch some porn while you try out your sex toys. For some couples, watching porn together is an enjoyable form of foreplay.

54 GO SKINNY-DIPPING

Everyone has heard of skinny-dipping, and some people may have even tried it when they were kids or teenagers. But have you done it with your significant other? If you can set up just the right conditions, now is the time to get stripping!

TIPS

- Similar to sex or lewdness in public, skinny-dipping in public is illegal in most places. It's risky to try to skinny-dip in public areas even if you think you're safe. A bit of a mood killer, I know, but there's no bigger mood killer than getting caught by the police.
- Don't have access to a private place to skinny-dip? Get in the shower together and try some role-playing.

TALK ABOUT IT

Talk about being naked. Would you visit a nudist resort? Why do you think people like or dislike being naked? Does being naked make you feel vulnerable or free?

SPEAK YOUR LOVE LANGUAGE

Tangential to the conversation about nakedness, you can also insert talk about what you love about your partner's body. As a gift, buy a sexy swimsuit for them to wear before or after you skinny-dip.

MAKE THE MOST OF IT

Don't just strip off your clothes, swim, and call it a night. Savor this evening, slow it down, and stretch it out. Make a romantic picnic. Drink wine, beer, or your favorite cocktail. Get cheese and crackers or other yummy snacks to eat before or after—or even when you take breaks from the water.

55 ROLE-PLAYING DATING

It can be exciting to pretend you're someone else from time to time. That's where role-playing comes in. Favorite characters in a romance novel? The hot electrician who comes by to service your lights just after you get out of the shower? You can become whoever you want!

TIPS

- Try a "strangers meeting" scenario for the chance to practice your seduction skills and explore your partner with fresh eyes.
- How about pretending to be a rock star spending the night with a gorgeous fan who caught their eye at a concert?

TALK ABOUT IT

If you are comfortable sharing this information with your partner, ask them about the riskiest sexual situation (in terms of roles) they have ever been in. Or, conversely, you can ask them what they fantasize about the most (even if it's never happened).

SPEAK YOUR LOVE LANGUAGE

Being vocal and descriptive with words can be exciting during role-play. Talk about your body parts and what you want to do with them. Give your partner a costume as a gift before you start role-playing.

MAKE THE MOST OF IT

It can be fun to take pictures of each other in your role-playing costumes. Take as many as you can during the role-playing. You can go back and look at them any time you feel horny and want to do it again. Unless you've agreed otherwise, photos are private and need to stay private between you and your partner. There's always the possibility of someone finding the images, so if you want the thrill of photography without the risk, you can always delete the images after your photo session.

56 PERSONAL SEX TAPE

When done safely in a committed relationship with mutual consent and privacy ground rules, recording yourself having sex with someone you trust can be exciting and educational. It's special because it helps you create and sustain a sexual connection.

TIPS

- Make sure no one else is home and that you don't expect anyone to drop by.
- Try to incorporate some of the other date ideas in this chapter (role-playing, fantasies, etc.) into your video.
- Keep safety and privacy in mind. You don't want anyone accidentally going through your phone and seeing your sex tape. If you're only in it for the thrill, you can record yourselves, watch the video, and delete it later for maximum security.

TALK ABOUT IT

Have a discussion ahead of time about what kinds of sexual activities you might like to see yourselves doing. Think about it—we don't usually get to see ourselves doing anything, let alone having sex. So, which activities would be the most exciting for you to watch yourselves doing on the screen?

SPEAK YOUR LOVE LANGUAGE

After you make the video, don't forget to watch it! It might be difficult for you or your partner to watch yourselves, so be very complimentary to your partner and their body. Many people have insecurities, so use your words to make each other feel loved and wanted.

MAKE THE MOST OF IT

If you are going to try to role-play, why not make up a whole story line for your sex video? It doesn't have to be long—just write your own script and direct and film a porn movie for your eyes only.

57 FULFILL EVERY FANTASY

Most people have sexual fantasies at one time or another. While some might be elaborate, specific, and ultra kinky, others might be general, less specific, and tamer. Whatever they may be, go on a date all about fulfilling your and your partner's sexual fantasies.

TIPS

- Maybe one of you has a fantasy to dominate—or to be dominated. Power play is a fantasy for many people.
- Pretend that you are stripper and you're giving your partner a private dance while you take your clothes off. Switch roles and have them do the same to you.
- Do some research online together to get inspiration, and you may find that the research itself is a major turn-on.

TALK ABOUT IT

Talk about all the sexual things you have ever wanted to try but have not had the opportunity (or the courage) to do. Then talk about the things you would *never, ever do*. This is important because it allows you to share your personal boundaries with your partner. Plus, it builds emotional intimacy as well.

SPEAK YOUR LOVE LANGUAGE

Why not write down your fantasies in full detail and give them as a gift to your partner on the date? This can be your own private erotica. Don't forget about words' power to turn your partner on!

MAKE THE MOST OF IT

Don't stick to just one fantasy. Try a few of them! Even if you can't do them all in one night, save some for later. This date is something that you can keep repeating as often as you like, so take advantage of it and don't forget to incorporate it into your normal sex life on occasion.

S&M: A PRIMER

If you tried the sex toy date and enjoyed it, maybe you'd like trying some S&M (sadomasochism), too. Think *Fifty Shades of Grey*. S&M isn't everyone's cup of tea, but it's certainly fun for a lot of people who want to test their sexual boundaries.

TIPS

- If one or both of you are new to S&M, you might want to read up on it together so that you know what you're getting into.
- Start with things that aren't too painful or uncomfortable, and work your way up to the more intense acts.
- Remember that you need to be careful with your partner to make sure you are not hurting them. Have a safe word—something they can say to tell you to stop if they want.

TALK ABOUT IT

It is important to talk about your boundaries ahead of time. How far do you want to go? What are your limits? What do you definitely want to try? What is your level of excitement or fear?

SPEAK YOUR LOVE LANGUAGE

Because a lot of S&M includes inflicting certain amounts of pain on your sexual partner, you need to be careful not to make things too unloving. Even though this might not be the way people usually imagine S&M, you can still show your affection with touch and/or words during your sex acts.

MAKE THE MOST OF IT

This date will probably require shopping for some sex props/toys, so why not buy some sexy S&M clothes, too? Create characters for yourselves and devise a sexual role-play narrative as you go along.

59

MARATHON SEX

Try to find a whole day to do nothing else but stay in bed (naked). Make love on and off throughout the day. Have a lazy, sexy, exciting all-day date!

TIPS

- Arrange for childcare or pet care if you need to. Try to get a whole day for yourselves, but if you can't, then at least spend a few hours on this date (maybe after your kids or pets go to bed early).
- Find favorite movies and/or TV shows to watch in between lovemaking. Make them romantic so that you can keep the mood going.
- Stock up on food and drinks of your choice so that you don't even have to get out of bed to eat. Sex burns calories, so you'll want to have light food to fuel up.

TALK ABOUT IT

Since this date is all about spending intimate time together for most of the day, the sky is literally the limit for what you can talk about. Buy a book full of questions ahead of time and choose from them at random. Try to talk about as many weird topics as you can, from alien abduction to what you would do if you won the lottery.

SPEAK YOUR LOVE LANGUAGE

This date is all about touching (obviously)! So, people who enjoy touch as an expression of love will be more than satisfied. You can also buy each other romantic gifts for the date—whether it's sexy lingerie or chocolates to feed each other.

MAKE THE MOST OF IT

Book a room (or a suite!) at a posh hotel for a night and stay in bed from check-in to check-out. Make a whole date out of finding pleasure in each other. Bring toys, props, sexy clothes, and anything else you can think of to make a memorable evening. Order room service that you can eat off each other. Then you can shower together to clean yourselves off.

7

GROUP DATES

While it's fun to go on dates alone with your partner, sometimes it's even more exciting when you double up with one or more couples. As the saying goes, "The more the merrier!"

If you are a new couple, you might be in the honeymoon phase where you want to spend all of your time together. While that's wonderful, it can also be isolating. And if you're in a long-term relationship or married, you might be stuck in a rut. Maybe when you were single, you did a lot of socializing with your friends. But since you've become a couple and maybe gotten married and had children, having fun with your friends might have fallen by the wayside. I get it; life happens to all of us.

Whatever point you may be at in your relationship, it is important not to neglect your friends. While it's great spending time alone with your partner, there is something about the energy of a group that can really make these dates memorable.

When you are out on the group dates in this chapter, don't forget to talk to everyone, including your partner. Some people can get lost in a group and go quiet. If you see that happening to someone, make an effort to draw them out of their shell. And if that someone is you, try to stay as engaged in the group as possible.

You can go on these dates with large groups or small groups. Big groups are fun, but sometimes having fewer people can foster more bonding. Regardless of the number of people involved, group dates can make for a lot of unforgettable memories.

TRIVIA NIGHT

Trivia games are a popular and time-honored tradition in our culture. Some people are more knowledgeable about useless (or not-so-useless) facts than others. Regardless, it's still fun to see how much you and your friends know. And even if you're not good at trivia, you can still learn something from your friends who do seem to know it all.

TIPS

- Many bars or restaurants hold trivia nights as a special event, so it shouldn't be hard to find a good place to go.
- If you don't want to go out or would rather compete just among yourselves, host a night for games like Trivial Pursuit at your home.
- Get creative and come up with your own trivia questions. You can find plenty of inspiration online for trivia categories. To avoid too many people at your trivia night knowing the questions beforehand, you may need to tap one person to serve as the official question-selector and reader/host.

TALK ABOUT IT

Trivia night sparks all kinds of great conversation. Since trivia topics can run the gamut, why not take breaks between rounds to discuss the facts that have come up in the game?

SPEAK YOUR LOVE LANGUAGE

Sit next to your partner and make sure you're on the same team (if you are playing on teams). Compliment your partner on how smart they are and how well they did in the game.

MAKE THE MOST OF IT

Add incentives to your trivia game. Every couple can buy a prize and bring it to the date. Make the prizes fun!

61 PLAY PAINTBALL

Paintball is a great group activity. It's active, competitive, and kicks your survival mode into gear. Find a nearby paintball venue and organize a friendly outing with your friends.

TIPS

- Gather a large enough group that you can have a field all to yourselves. That way, you won't have to play against strangers.
- Divide your group into teams and compete to see who will win the "war."

TALK ABOUT IT

This game activates a survival mode in us that pushes us to outlast our competitors and be the last person standing. Talk about how to survive in the wilderness. What would you bring? What skills do you think you would need to survive? How long do you think you could last?

SPEAK YOUR LOVE LANGUAGE

In order to bond, make sure that you're on the same team as your partner. In fact, everyone should be on the same team as their partner. The whole point of dates is to bond—not to be each other's enemies. Having a common goal to take down another couple? Well, that can also strengthen your bond, but remember and communicate to one another that this date is meant to be harmless fun among friends.

MAKE THE MOST OF IT

Don't just stop at paintball. You'll most likely be going on this date during the daytime, so carry the fun on into the night. Go out for dinner and/or drinks afterward. That'll help shake off the sense of competition and get everyone back on the same team. Find a place with live music to listen to, and relax for the rest of the evening.

62 SING YOUR HEARTS OUT

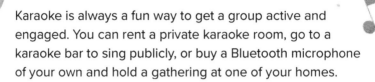

Karaoke is always a fun way to get a group active and engaged. You can rent a private karaoke room, go to a karaoke bar to sing publicly, or buy a Bluetooth microphone of your own and hold a gathering at one of your homes.

TIPS

- Make this date into a singing contest. Everyone should sing their favorite song(s), and at the end of the night, everyone should vote for their favorite singer.
- Decide on a prize for the winner. It could be free drinks, dinner, or a bottle of their favorite champagne.
- Form two "bands" and have a battle! Make things more challenging by having the other band pick the song your group needs to sing.

TALK ABOUT IT

Does anyone in the group have stage fright? Give one another tips on how to overcome it, and make sure to encourage one another when you are performing (especially if it's in front of strangers).

SPEAK YOUR LOVE LANGUAGE

If your partner is nervous about singing, use positive words to encourage them. Tell them they have a good voice and that you are proud of them for being courageous. Hold hands and sit next to each other during the karaoke performances. Perform in a duet together so that your partner feels less alone.

MAKE THE MOST OF IT

Instead of just following one of the tips above, why not do them all? Have a whole night of singing with contests, a diva sing-off, dueling bands, and couples performing romantic duets. Buy gold medal party favors or little trophies as prizes for the night.

63 WHITE ELEPHANT PARTY

If you aren't familiar with what a white elephant party is, here are the rules. Every person buys a gift (for no one in particular) to bring to the party. One person starts the festivities by opening one of the gifts. Then a second person opens a gift and makes a choice: They can either keep it or steal the first person's gift. After that, a third person opens a gift and faces the same choice—only now they can steal from either the first or second person. If your gift is stolen, you can pick from the remaining unopened gifts or steal someone else's to replace it, potentially setting off a chain reaction. The game continues until the last person has opened their gift and the last potential chain of steals has reached its conclusion.

TIPS

- Choose gifts generic enough for any gender and age.
- Or, you can decide as a group to get wacky, funny gifts. This makes for a hilarious time!
- Set a gift budget and have everyone stick to it. You don't want one person to bring a $100 bottle of wine while another person gives someone a cheap keychain.

TALK ABOUT IT

Take turns talking about the best and the worst gifts you have ever been given.

SPEAK YOUR LOVE LANGUAGE

Just because you're buying gifts to bring to the party doesn't mean you can't buy your partner a more meaningful, romantic gift at the same time. Be of service to your partner and refill their drink or plate of snacks.

MAKE THE MOST OF IT

Most people do white elephant gift exchanges around Christmas, but you don't have to wait if you don't want to! You can host a white elephant party any time of the year.

64   FIND NEW TUNES

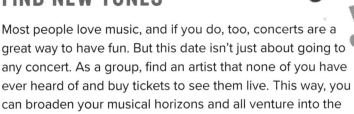

Most people love music, and if you do, too, concerts are a great way to have fun. But this date isn't just about going to any concert. As a group, find an artist that none of you have ever heard of and buy tickets to see them live. This way, you can broaden your musical horizons and all venture into the performance on the same level.

TIPS

- Everyone should do a little research and write down the name of a band they hadn't heard of before. The band should be currently active and having an upcoming local performance. Randomly choose one from a bucket. That's your upcoming concert.
- After you choose a band to see, find some of their music online to familiarize yourself a little. Concerts are always more fun when you know some of the music!

TALK ABOUT IT

Name the top five concerts you've ever been to. Why did you like them so much? What are some of the worst concerts you've ever been to? Why were they so bad? What would be your dream concert?

SPEAK YOUR LOVE LANGUAGE

A concert is a great place to hold hands or put your arms around each other. Buy your partner a T-shirt or some other tour merchandise to remember the experience. Make sure to check if your partner is comfortable; concerts can be exhausting!

MAKE THE MOST OF IT

Don't just go to the concert. Make a whole experience out of it! Wear concert T-shirts and go out for dinner and/or drinks before the show. Make it a memorable evening with friends!

65 CASINO NIGHT

Gambling is a fun way to spend an evening among friends. Even if you don't have a lot of money, you can still feel the thrill of trying to beat the odds and win. See who will pay up and who will win it all!

TIPS

- At the casino, make sure you all play the same game at the same time. That's the point of the date—to hang out and be together.
- If you don't live near a casino, you can host a casino night at someone's home. You can stick to poker chips and card games or splash out and rent slot machines, a roulette wheel, a casino table—whatever you want to try.

TALK ABOUT IT

Talk to each other about what you like and don't like about gambling. What is your favorite game? What is your least favorite game? You can also talk about the lottery (which is a form of gambling). Discuss what you would do if you won millions of dollars one day.

SPEAK YOUR LOVE LANGUAGE

If you win some money, use it to buy a special gift. This could be an individual gift for your partner or one that you give to yourselves as a couple. If you're at the casino, stay close to your partner so that you can hold hands while you gamble and spend the evening together.

MAKE THE MOST OF IT

Even though this date is all about gambling, don't forget to mix in some food, drink, and music! If you decide to go to a casino, you could even stay overnight or go big on a couples' weekend in Las Vegas.

66 GROUP THRILL RIDERS

If your group is into extremes, try going to an amusement park to ride every single roller coaster. This is a fun way to experience a group thrill.

TIPS

- You might have some people in your group who are afraid to go on certain rides. Make bets beforehand on who will go on every ride and who will chicken out.
- Go on this date at night. The loops and drops of a roller coaster are even more exciting in the dark!
- You can also take a break from the extreme rides to see a show, play arcade games, or ride go-karts and bumper cars.

TALK ABOUT IT

Ask your group what their fears are regarding extreme amusement park rides. Are they afraid of death? Do they not like the feeling of free-falling? Do the rides go too fast? Conversely, talk about what you all love about the rides. You can even recount some funny childhood memories from when you went to amusement parks with your parents.

SPEAK YOUR LOVE LANGUAGE

Extreme rides can be scary for a lot of people, so don't forget to sit with your partner and hold hands if possible. This reaffirms your love for and protection of each other. Buy ride photos of you as a couple and of your whole group to remember the fun date.

MAKE THE MOST OF IT

If this is a close-knit group of friends, try turning this date into a road trip! Map out the amusement parks within a few hours' drive. Then take a long weekend and go to as many as you possibly can.

A PROGRESSIVE DINNER PARTY

If you all live in the same city, a progressive dinner party is a fun date idea for a group. Ideally, your party will have at least four stops. You could start at one home for a cocktail with appetizers, go to another for soup and salad, move to the next for the main course, and end the evening with dessert and after-dinner drinks at your final destination.

TIPS

- This will take some planning and coordinating, both in terms of food and timing. Work together to create an itinerary to make sure everyone is on the same page.
- Each home should plan a fun activity to go along with the food or drink they are providing to guests.
- Try selecting an overarching theme for the evening. For example, you could turn the event into a dance party. Each home would play a different genre of music.

TALK ABOUT IT

Focus your conversation on the theme of the night. For example, if you decide to play a different genre of music at every home, talk about your favorite artists in each genre. Or have a dance-off to see who has the hottest dance moves.

SPEAK YOUR LOVE LANGUAGE

You and your partner can spend quality time together preparing and planning your part of this progressive date. And don't forget to be affectionate with each other as you are driving to each home (and while you're there).

MAKE THE MOST OF IT

Dress up according to the evening's theme. The sky's the limit for what you can dream up for this fun group date.

68 PAINT NIGHT PARTY

Exercising your creative muscles is refreshing and fun even if you think you don't have a creative bone in your body. Easy-to-follow instructions make this date great for beginners or anyone who wants to hold a wineglass and a paintbrush.

TIPS

- Paint nights are a popular business, so find a studio or event space where you and your friends can buy tickets to one. The venue will provide the materials; all you'll need to bring is yourself (and, depending on the venue, maybe your own drinks).
- No local paint night studio? No problem! You can buy tickets to a virtual event instead, along with kits containing all the supplies you need: canvas, easels, paint, and so on. Host your group at your place or a friend's place and paint together.
- Most studios encourage you to bring food. Whether you're all getting dinner together beforehand, preparing plenty of snacks to bring to the studio, or hosting your own virtual night, make a food plan.

TALK ABOUT IT

A paint night party can be a gateway to conversations about the arts. What are your favorite museums? Do you have a favorite artist? Is there a destination museum on your travel bucket list?

SPEAK YOUR LOVE LANGUAGE

Bring a favorite food or drink as a surprise gift for your partner. Offer acts of service, like refilling your partner's drink cup and getting more food for their snack plate.

MAKE THE MOST OF IT

Come to your paint night party in costume! You can coordinate an outfit with your partner and dress as two famous artists.

69 PUT ON YOUR OWN PLAY

It's time to get creative! As a group, write a short script for you all to act out. Make it a comedy to keep the mood light and you can laugh all night. The funnier, the better.

TIPS

- As a group, come up with the overall story line. If you're having writer's block, a great idea is to take a show or movie you all love and create a parody of it. Each person can take a character and contribute their lines. You can even write in additional characters—anything you want!
- Don't forget about costumes and props. Be creative with whatever you have on hand. It'll only add to the humor.
- Assign one person to be the "Academy Awards" judge. They'll watch the play, then award "Oscars" for best actor and actress.

TALK ABOUT IT

Talk about your favorite plays. Make recommendations for others in your group. Then pull out your calendars and find a time to see some of them together.

SPEAK YOUR LOVE LANGUAGE

Compliment your partner on their creativity and acting skills. Flirt during your performance if you have lines together. Perform an act of service by helping them write their lines.

MAKE THE MOST OF IT

Are you ready to take the skills you gained from your stage production to the next level? Why not try out for a local theater production? You may or may not all make it into the actual cast, but you can still be part of the show by designing costumes, lighting, or sound, managing ticket sales, or any other roles suited to your skills.

70

SUPER DATE

A MASQUERADE BALL

Masquerade balls first became popular in 16th-century Venice, Italy, and spread across Europe in the following centuries. In modern times, the spirit lives on—even if you haven't attended a masquerade ball yourself, you have probably seen parties where everyone dresses up in black-tie attire and wears an ornate mask in movies or on TV. *The Phantom of the Opera* includes an iconic masquerade ball scene, and *Fifty Shades of Grey* also features one.

TIPS

- Depending on how many couples are involved, you might want to consider renting a small banquet facility for this date. If you have a large guest list, you may want to enlist help for the planning and organization, too.
- Decorate the place where you are having the party, regardless of whether it is a home or a public venue.
- Have a costume contest. Give an award at the end of the night to the best-dressed couple.

TALK ABOUT IT

Have a conversation about metaphorical masks. Is there something about yourself (or something you have done) that you have hidden from others? If so, what is that thing? And why have you hidden it? Go as deep as you want to on this topic.

SPEAK YOUR LOVE LANGUAGE

A masquerade ball is a perfect time to get all dressed up for your partner, so don't forget to tell each other how sexy you look in your black-tie attire. Wow your partner with the gift of jewelry or fancy cufflinks to wear to the ball. Keep your arms around each other and hold hands as much as you can throughout the night. Make sure to pull out chairs for each other, hold out arms for support, and perform other small acts of service.

MAKE THE MOST OF IT

If you're going to go big, hire a party planner. It's well worth the money to find someone else to manage your massive event so that you can spend your time actually enjoying the festivities. Get party favors and props to hand out to attendees, including boas, crowns, tiaras, and feathers. Also, organize some games to play at the party, such as musical chairs or a treasure hunt.

(8)

HOLIDAYS & SPECIAL OCCASIONS

It's normal, and even expected, for couples to celebrate holidays and special occasions together. But you might not have thought about turning them into bucket list dates with your significant other.

This chapter is all about using the special days on the calendar to find inspiration for your memorable bucket list dates.

Most people celebrate the major holidays like Christmas, Hannukah, Thanksgiving, or Easter. Many people choose to spend these days with extended family, while others like to have a more quiet, intimate experience. Regardless of how you usually celebrate, you can always turn these days into bucket list dates to remember.

As for myself, up until recent years, I always spent holidays with my extended family. However, as my children grew up into adulthood, there was a need to rethink how we all celebrated. For us, we got to the point where we celebrated major holidays like Christmas early.

At first, it was a big adjustment. But after a while, my partner and I realized that it was a great opportunity to do our own thing! It was very exciting to see the lights and music of Nashville, Tennessee, on Christmas Day and to bond with other couples who were also spending the holidays in a less traditional manner.

In order to have a great experience going on the dates in this chapter, you need to break out of your traditional ways of doing things. I encourage you to look at the calendar and let it guide you into doing something really special together.

It isn't always easy to do something out of the ordinary, but it is definitely worth it because you will create memories that last a lifetime.

71 ALL HALLOWS' EVE EVENT

Halloween is always a fun time of year because you can get creative and creepy all at the same time. If you have never thrown a party for this particular holiday, now is your chance to do it and have a lot of fun with your partner along the way!

TIPS

- Dress up in couple's costumes. Some ideas include Bonnie and Clyde, peanut butter and jelly, or Clark Kent/Superman and Lois Lane.
- Turn your party into a murder mystery game and let your friends try to solve the whodunit.
- Gross out your guests with a "feel" box. Put all sorts of weird slimy objects in there and ask your guests to guess what they are without looking—only feeling.

TALK ABOUT IT

Since Halloween is all about the creepy and the supernatural, ask each other (or the group) if you believe in ghosts. Has anyone ever seen one or felt one? Do you know anyone who has?

SPEAK YOUR LOVE LANGUAGE

If you don't feel like dressing up in a couple's costume, you can surprise each other by buying costumes as a gift. Answer the door together for trick-or-treaters.

MAKE THE MOST OF IT

Make your event into a haunted Halloween party. Scare each other (and your guests) with dramatic retellings of scary stories with a flashlight. Have a friend hide and make loud ghost noises or dress up in a werewolf or vampire costume and suddenly pop out to scare everyone.

SERVING THOSE IN NEED ON THANKSGIVING

Thanksgiving is not just about eating turkey and stuffing. It should be a day where you give genuine thanks for everything you have in your life. It is a perfect day to serve those who are less fortunate than you by helping feed people in a homeless shelter.

TIPS

- Plan ahead of time so that you know where and when you will go. A lot of people choose to volunteer on Thanksgiving, so be sure to call shelters ahead of the holiday. You can pick a shift either before or after your own celebration.
- Don't just hand out food; talk to the people whom you are serving. They have stories to tell. If they're willing to share, listen.

TALK ABOUT IT

Talk about the things you are most grateful for. Unfortunately, most people don't take the time to identify the good things in their lives—even on Thanksgiving. So, make sure you focus on your blessings in a conversation on your date.

SPEAK YOUR LOVE LANGUAGE

This date is all about words of affirmation. Don't just talk about general things you are thankful for in life; remember to also talk about what you love about your partner and how much they mean to you.

MAKE THE MOST OF IT

Why not make volunteering a permanent part of your lives together? Not only is giving to others something you can do together, but it will also make you feel good about yourselves as individuals and a couple.

73 FIREWORKS ON INDEPENDENCE DAY

Many people like to see fireworks on Independence Day; why not make the spectacle into a bucket list date? Instead of just going to your local fireworks display, travel to a city that has a huge fireworks show.

TIPS

- Choose a city that is well-known for its fireworks display. For example, Chicago has fireworks on the evening of July 3rd as part of its Taste of Chicago event, New York has the Macy's 4th of July Fireworks show, and Boston has the Boston Pops Orchestra perform live with its fireworks display.
- Plan ahead and make sure you take in all the sights of the city you choose to see the fireworks in.
- If you would rather stay at home, host your very own private 4th of July party with party favors and a good old-fashioned barbecue.

TALK ABOUT IT

Independence Day is all about freedom. What does freedom mean to you? Extend the concept to all areas of your life. How much freedom do you want in your relationship? In your career? In your life?

SPEAK YOUR LOVE LANGUAGE

Sit close and hold hands as you watch the fireworks. If touring a city, you can buy little souvenirs for each other.

MAKE THE MOST OF IT

If you want to get adventurous, you can turn this bucket list date into a road trip. After you choose the final destination where you want to watch the fireworks, map out some other places along the way that are of historical significance or just plain interesting to see.

74 INTERNATIONAL DAY OF HAPPINESS

The United Nations designated March 20th as a day to celebrate the importance of happiness in our lives and because happiness should be a fundamental human right for all. It also established 17 Sustainable Development Goals to identify the key global changes needed to increase happiness worldwide. Spend the day in service to others with these goals in mind.

TIPS

- Identify ways you can spend the day performing acts of service toward achieving these goals. For example, you could find items in good condition in your home that you no longer use and donate them to a charity supporting impoverished families.
- Whether you spend the whole day or part of the day with your partner, chart out a plan for how to maximize your long-term impact on spreading sustainable happiness together.

TALK ABOUT IT

How often do you perform community service, and would you like to make it a greater part of your life? What are the social and economic issues that you are most passionate about?

SPEAK YOUR LOVE LANGUAGE

It'll be a busy day, but that doesn't mean you won't have opportunities to speak your love languages. Perform acts of service for each other, particularly if you're doing physically demanding work. Steal glances at each other across the room and smile. Whisper words of affection in your partner's ear during the course of the day.

MAKE THE MOST OF IT

Commit yourselves to these acts of service for more than just a day; find a way to make them a sustainable and routine part of your life.

75 RANDOM ACTS OF KINDNESS DAY

February 17th is Random Acts of Kindness Day in the United States. There's little that sparks more joy than surprising someone with an act of kindness, like giving up your seat on the train, paying for the coffee of next person behind you, or buying a hot meal for a homeless person. You never know how a single act can transform the life of another person. Spend all day with your partner creatively "committing" acts of kindness.

TIPS

- The spirit of the holiday is "random," but you can still make a plan and challenge yourselves to perform a certain number of acts of kindness throughout the day.
- February 17th might fall on a weekday when you and your partner are both at work or school, but you can still spend the day "together" by texting each other about your acts.
- Plan to end your day together with a special act of kindness for each other. Think of something that would be meaningful and joyful to your partner.

TALK ABOUT IT

How did it feel to surprise people with your acts of kindness? Trade stories of the reactions you received, if you were able to witness them, throughout your day.

SPEAK YOUR LOVE LANGUAGE

Make dinner for your partner. Compliment their creativity on their acts of kindness. Express how you feel about seeing your partner's generosity. Tell your partner how meaningful it was to devote a date to helping others.

MAKE THE MOST OF IT

Make this more than a holiday and transform it into a lifestyle. Can you challenge yourselves to perform at least one random act of kindness a day?

76 APRIL FOOLS' JOKES

For anyone who likes pranks, April Fools' Day (April 1st) is the perfect occasion for a crazy, fun date that will keep you and your partner laughing all day (and night).

TIPS

- Paint a bar of soap with clear nail polish and put it in your shower.
- If you use ice cube trays, fill them with lemon-lime soda instead of water so that the next time someone uses them they will wonder what's wrong with their drink.

TALK ABOUT IT

Talk about the funniest things you have experienced in your lives. What are boundaries of humor for you? Observe your partner carefully on this date to make sure none of your pranks cross the line. What one person might think is harmless could be interpreted as quite harmful by another. If you think you've gone too far, ask your partner. Apologize if you have and pull back on the pranks.

SPEAK YOUR LOVE LANGUAGE

Despite the nature of the holiday, April Fools' Day is still a day when you can let your partner know how much they mean to you and show your affection with a hug, a kiss, or maybe more. End the day with surprise gifts for each other that help close the page on the pranks and remind you both of your closeness.

MAKE THE MOST OF IT

While most people pull pranks on April Fools' Day, you don't necessarily need to wait until April 1st to go on this bucket list date. You can pull pranks any time you want—just make sure that your partner is receptive to this type of humor.

OUR YEAR IN REVIEW

New Year's Eve is always a sentimental day. It's a time to look back at all you did throughout the year and cherish the memories. So it's a great occasion to make a commemorative video of your journey as a couple through part of or the whole year.

TIPS

- Both of you should choose your favorite pictures of the two of you from throughout the year. Find as many as you can.
- Pick music that you both like to put in the video. Find songs that came out that year.
- Sit down together with your photos and music and arrange them chronologically. You can also include videos as well. You can find apps that make it easy to compile everything together.

TALK ABOUT IT

Stroll down memory lane and tell each other about the best and worst New Year's Eves you've ever had. What made the best one so good? What made the worst one so bad? What would be your ideal way to spend New Year's in the future?

SPEAK YOUR LOVE LANGUAGE

Buy each other little end-of-the-year gifts. Make sure to thank your partner for all the things they did for you throughout the year. Congratulate them on getting through the year.

MAKE THE MOST OF IT

In addition to the pictures that you are putting in your video, record end-of-the-year messages to each other to add at the end. Try to not let your partner see your video message until after the final video is done. In your message, tell your partner what you love about them and your favorite memories of them from that year.

NEW YEAR'S EVE BASH

New Year's Eve is always the biggest, splashiest celebration of the year. The New Year brings a clean slate, a new dawn, and the perfect opportunity to party with your sweetie! Instead of having a quiet evening at home, this bucket list date is all about finding a big New Year's Eve party to go to. The energy of a large group as you're counting down to the New Year is exhilarating!

TIPS

- Most large hotels will hold a New Year's Eve party for their guests and others in town who want to attend.
- If you'd rather not go to a hotel celebration, there are many other venues that hold New Year's Eve parties, such as restaurants, bars, concert venues, and nightclubs.

TALK ABOUT IT

Talk about the New Year's resolutions that you have made in years gone by. How many of them did you stick with long term? Which ones did you fail to keep? What kinds of resolutions do you want to make this year, and what can you do to make sure you keep them? How can you support your partner to help them keep their resolutions?

SPEAK YOUR LOVE LANGUAGE

This can be a very romantic date, so why not buy flowers, cologne, or lingerie to commemorate the New Year? Also, don't forget to be affectionate with each other in your words and actions as you reflect on the year that just ended.

MAKE THE MOST OF IT

Make this a destination celebration. Cruise ships always have a big party for New Year's Eve, and you can probably find a lot of other destinations that offer a New Year's package including a big celebration as well.

79 BYO HOLIDAY

Why celebrate all the regular holidays when you could build your own? On this date, you'll create a special day just for the two of you. It is romantic because it is only for you.

TIPS

- Choose a date together. It can be one that is either already special (such as your anniversary) or a completely random date on the calendar.
- Combine elements from two different holidays, such as eating a Thanksgiving dinner while dressed up in a Halloween costume.
- Make up "holiday rules." For example, on Christmas you kiss under the mistletoe, and on Halloween you eat a lot of candy and dress up. Try creating, mixing, and matching holiday rules of your very own.

TALK ABOUT IT

Take time to talk about your favorite holiday memories. Why did you like those times so much? Did you ever have a holiday that was "disastrous" but in a funny way?

SPEAK YOUR LOVE LANGUAGE

Make gift giving a part of your special holiday to show your partner that you care and that you put thought into getting them something. Perform acts of service while you are preparing for the holiday to share the load with your partner.

MAKE THE MOST OF IT

Instead of making this date just an annual occurrence, create several special holidays so that you can enjoy them every few months. That way, you don't have to wait around for the next big date on the calendar because you already have your own!

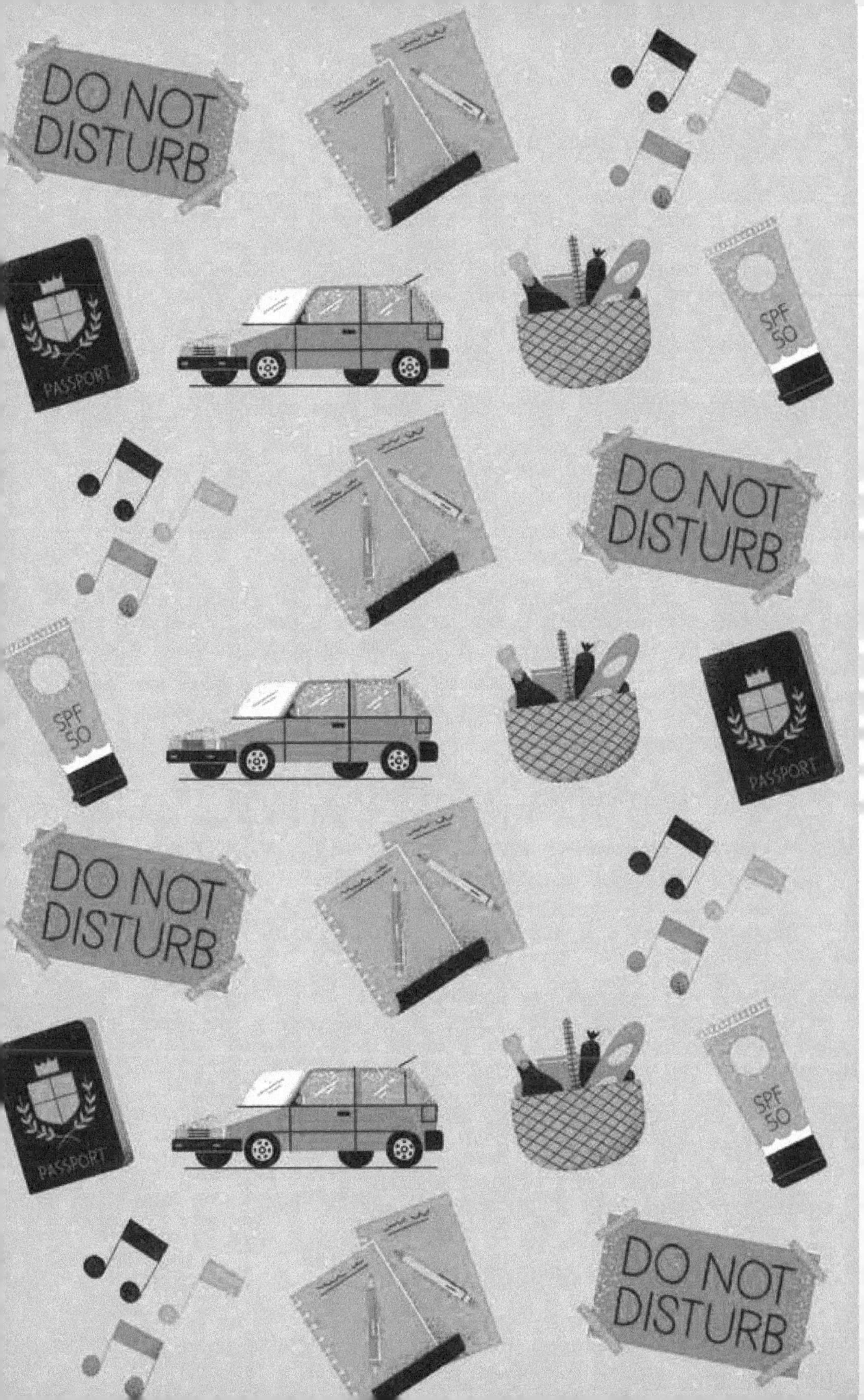
DO NOT DISTURB
PASSPORT
SPF 50

80

VALENTINE'S DAY SCAVENGER HUNT

Valentine's Day is the holiday of love, so of course it makes sense to turn it into a bucket list date! On this date, each of you will put together a scavenger hunt for the other to complete. Pick a starting point and leave a note there with a clue on how to find the next one. At the end of the scavenger hunt, have a Valentine's gift waiting for your partner.

TIPS

- With each clue, write down one of your favorite memories of being a couple.
- You could also put romantic quotes on each clue along with explanations of why you chose them and why they make you think of your partner.
- Instead of just leaving clues, you can leave small prizes or gifts for your partner at each point on your scavenger hunt. Then, at the end of the hunt, they will find their big present.

TALK ABOUT IT

Talk about what "love" means to you both. What does it look like, and what do you expect and want from it? You may or may not be at the "love" stage of your relationship, but talking about love is important in any relationship. Also, discuss what celebrating holidays together means to you. What does it mean to mark a special occasion together?

SPEAK YOUR LOVE LANGUAGE

If you follow the tips above, you will compliment each other in your clues with words of affirmation. Also, don't forget to be physically affectionate with each other—after all, it is Valentine's Day!

MAKE THE MOST OF IT

While you could do this date at home, it would also be fun to
do it in an outdoor place like a park or the woods. That way,
the scavenger hunt will be a little more challenging. Just don't
forget where you put your clues and gifts! You can also create
a scrapbook together out of the clues that have your favorite
memories and quotes written down.

9

FOOD, ARTS & CULTURE

Are you ready to taste new food, learn about other cultures, and try your hand at making art? Maybe you've always wanted to but just haven't had the time yet. Well, now is your chance to explore all of these things and more in some really fun bucket list dates.

Learning more about another culture through its celebrations is a rewarding experience in itself. From participating in new traditions to tasting new foods, experiencing and learning new things together can also be a bonding experience for a couple. You'll learn a great deal about each other when you approach something together as beginners.

Are there foods that you've always wanted to try but haven't yet? Or foods that you've tasted at a restaurant and want to learn to make at home? Can you distinguish one type of wine from another? Or taste how different styles of brewing produce vastly different results? Now is the time to stretch your palate and experience new tastes with some good food and drinks.

If you have a taste for the finer things in life, then this chapter is for you! These bucket list dates help you discover new favorites and broader horizons.

81 OKTOBERFEST

Oktoberfest is an annual two-week celebration that originated in Munich, Germany, in 1810. As the years went by, many other countries started holding their own Oktoberfest festivities. Today, there's a good chance you can find an Oktoberfest celebration right in your own hometown (or nearby).

TIPS

- Give yourselves a little history lesson by doing some research on the original Oktoberfest before you attend one. You'll better appreciate the experience when you understand the origins of this festival.
- If you like beer, taste several varieties at Oktoberfest so that you can find new flavors you love and expand your preferences.
- Try new foods that you maybe haven't even heard of before. There is always something unique available for every taste.

TALK ABOUT IT

Talk about how you would create your own festival based on your cultural upbringing. What traditions are important to you to celebrate? What foods would you serve and what performances would attendees see?

SPEAK YOUR LOVE LANGUAGE

As you walk around Oktoberfest, hold hands or put your arms around each other. Surprise your partner with a handmade German gift from one of the festival vendors. This would be a great way to remember your bucket list date.

MAKE THE MOST OF IT

You don't have to stick to going to just one Oktoberfest. You could make it a month-long bucket list date by going to as many Oktoberfest celebrations as you can find. And get creative—try making your own beer!

82 TAKE A SPIN ON THE POTTERY WHEEL

If you have ever seen the movie *Ghost,* you know how sexy pottery can be! There is just something about getting your hands all goopy and sloppy that makes it fun. So why not turn it into a date?

TIPS

- Find a nearby pottery studio with a simple Google search. You may be surprised to discover that you've walked or driven by one many times without even realizing it was there.
- Think about what you want to make before you go. Choose something that you can use as a couple.
- If you've spent time behind a pottery wheel before, challenge yourself to make something new.

TALK ABOUT IT

Pottery is a great activity because you can talk about anything while you sit at the wheel sculpting side by side. Clay is one of the oldest building materials. Talk about pottery from other cultures that you have learned about. Which styles are the most interesting to you and why? Would you like to see more historical examples of pottery? Where would you go?

SPEAK YOUR LOVE LANGUAGE

You can have a little fun with touch while you are making your pottery. Tease each other by getting your faces dirty, and talk about how cute your partner looks when they're covered in mud.

MAKE THE MOST OF IT

Rent or buy a pottery wheel if you want to re-create that romantic scene from *Ghost* at home. Turn the lights down low, light candles, play music, and see how messy you can get.

83 FIND A FOOD FESTIVAL

If you enjoy good food, then walking around nibbling dishes from a variety of specialty food vendors would be a perfect date for you. Find a local food festival you can attend, and make a date fit for foodies.

TIPS

- Research what food festivals happen in your area, and make a plan to go to the next upcoming one that whets both of your appetites.
- If beer or wine are of interest to you, consider expanding your search to include beer and wine festivals.
- Can't find a local food festival? Make your own with a local tour of food trucks in your area. Map out a walking or a driving plan, and spend the day eating your way through your very own food truck crawl.

TALK ABOUT IT

They say food is the language of love, and there's no better time to talk about food than on this date. What are your favorite foods? Do you have a favorite memory around food? What do you enjoy cooking at home? What are your comfort foods?

SPEAK YOUR LOVE LANGUAGE

Hold hands while you walk around the festival. Offer a taste of your food to your partner and feed them. Tell your partner how much you enjoy their company and finding new and fun things to do together.

MAKE THE MOST OF IT

Shoot for the moon and make a plan to attend one (or more) of the ultimate bucket list food festivals. Perhaps PoutineFest in Ottawa, Canada; Pizzafest in Naples, Italy; or the National Cherry Festival in Traverse City, Michigan? Let your stomachs guide you as you plan a foodie's vacation.

84 GO TO A RENAISSANCE FESTIVAL

From the opulent clothes to the knights and sword fights, a Renaissance faire can take you back to a fascinating time in history. It's like stepping into a time machine!

TIPS

- Instead of just going in your jeans and T-shirt, buy or rent costumes so that you can really feel like you are living in a different century.
- If you're married, you could renew your wedding vows on this date—many Renaissance festivals have a gazebo where they perform weddings.

TALK ABOUT IT

Since this bucket list date is about exploring a different time in history, talk about whether or not either of you would use a time machine if you could. If so, where would you go? Would you still go if there was only a 50 percent chance that you could return to the present moment afterward? What if you could come back, but everything would be different in the present moment because the timeline had changed?

SPEAK YOUR LOVE LANGUAGE

If you dress up in costumes, compliment your partner on how sexy they look in their medieval attire. Hold hands as you walk around the festival. Feed each other.

MAKE THE MOST OF IT

It is fun to go on this date during the winter holiday season because you might also be able to find madrigal singers or a Renaissance-style choir performing in your area around the same time. At this time of year, there's usually also a feast to go along with the entertainment. You can do the festival during the day and the madrigal performance by night!

85 VINEYARD VOYAGE

Many people love wine, but how often do people take the opportunity to learn more about winemaking and the seemingly infinite number of varieties of this drink? This date goes beyond just ordering a glass of vino with your meal at a restaurant. Plan a trip to a vineyard to take a deep dive into the tasty nuances of the humble and delicious grape.

TIPS

- If you can find a nearby vineyard to visit, take a tour there to learn about how wine is made—and specifically how it's made at that particular vineyard. Every vineyard has its own unique practices.
- Arrive at the tasting room with a clean palate.
- Wine is a sophisticated drink, so dress your best. Dressing up for each other also makes the date more special.

TALK ABOUT IT

Think about a year that you would like to mark with a wine bottle of that vintage. What year would you like to "store" in a bottle and open up later? Would it taste bitter? Sweet? Sour? Why do you want to store that particular year?

SPEAK YOUR LOVE LANGUAGE

Wine can be very romantic, so sit next to each other and hold hands. You can even intertwine your arms and drink your wine together. Buy your partner their favorite bottle of wine as a gift when the wine tasting is over.

MAKE THE MOST OF IT

You don't need to go out to a winery or vineyard to have a wine tasting bucket list date. You can do it at home and make it a very intimate event. Buy a wide variety of wines, then set up your own tasting by candlelight.

86 DO A PUB CRAWL

Pretend that you're back in college and spend a day or evening on a pub crawl! Hit up a variety of restaurants and bars for a wide selection of drinks and food.

TIPS

- Leave your car at home and make sure your preferred rideshare app is up-to-date on your phone. You don't want to drink and drive, so request cars to take you from one pub to the next.
- Map out where you are going beforehand so that you don't waste time trying to figure out where to go next.
- If you want spontaneity, head for a neighborhood with plenty of options within walking distance, then just let the wind take you to your next stop.

TALK ABOUT IT

Most people have a "party story" to tell, but you might not have shared yours with your partner yet. This is the perfect time to share. Did you throw a huge party in high school? What's the worst drink you've ever had? You can literally talk about anything—the good, the bad, and even the ugly!

SPEAK YOUR LOVE LANGUAGE

Don't forget to sit next to each other and hold hands at each bar or pub. Ditto for when you are walking around. Remind your partner how attractive you think they are, and talk about some fun things you can do when you get home (wink, wink!).

MAKE THE MOST OF IT

Many large cities sponsor pub crawl tours. You can pedal a beer trolley with other patrons or ride in a horse-drawn carriage from location to location. This option adds a little adventure, whimsy, and romance to your bucket list date.

87 ANTIQUING FOR TREASURE

You might already be an antique lover and not yet know it. Do you enjoy searching for unique statement furniture or one-of-a-kind pieces of jewelry? Do you like architectural styles from the past? If you answered yes, then there is an antiquer in you! You never know what precious gem you will find in an antique shop.

TIPS

- Choose an antique item that you would like to find, then make a game of it. Whoever finds it first wins.
- Keep your eye out for something you think your partner will love, and surprise them with it as a gift later.
- Challenge yourselves to see who can find the oldest item.

TALK ABOUT IT

When you find interesting antiques, make up stories about them. For instance, if you find an old milk can from the 1920s, create a story about the family who owned it first. Each of you can add to the overall narrative as you go along. It's a fun way to get your creative juices flowing.

SPEAK YOUR LOVE LANGUAGE

As suggested above, buy your partner a special antique as a gift. Pay close attention and try to find something that will be really significant to them based on how well you know your partner. Hold hands while you walk around admiring all the antiques.

MAKE THE MOST OF IT

Choose a room in your home to redecorate in a new period style or to give new life with key pieces from your antiquing discoveries. This will give you both something to focus on while you shop and a project you can enjoy completing together when you return from this bucket list date.

INTERNATIONAL BREWERY OR DISTILLERY TOUR

If you're curious about how things are made, check out a brewery or a distillery tour. Most major cities have breweries and distilleries that offer tours and even sampling as you go along. To make this date even more exciting, consider a trip to Scotland to try whiskey and haggis in the place where they originated.

TIPS

- Pay special attention when you taste the beers or liquors. Many places allow you to purchase your favorites.
- If you do buy your favorite beer or whiskey, make a special dinner to accompany it.

TALK ABOUT IT

Add some history to your conversations. There was a time in the early 1900s when alcohol use was against the law: Prohibition. If you don't know much about it, look up some facts and read up together. Ask each other "what if" questions like: What if Prohibition happened now?

SPEAK YOUR LOVE LANGUAGE

Make sure that you are affectionate with each other on the tour. If your partner is indecisive about buying something, sneak around them and get it so that you can surprise them later.

MAKE THE MOST OF IT

Try to find as many tours in the same city as you can. Schedule them ahead of time so that you can fit in as many as possible in one day. If you're in Scotland, you're in luck: There are 130 malt and grain distilleries in this country, which is the densest concentration anywhere in the world.

89 A NEW CELEBRATION

Take a trip to another country during a national celebration or holiday. It's a festive and exciting way to experience another culture and learn about their traditions.

TIPS

- You could go to Pamplona, Spain, in July and attend one of Spain's most iconic festivals, Fiesta de San Fermín, where you can experience the running of the bulls.
- Greenland is the perfect place to visit on June 21st, the summer solstice, which is the longest day of the year. On this date, Greenland's National Day is celebrated with a summer festival.
- If you can't travel, try re-creating a holiday at home.

TALK ABOUT IT

What culture in the world interests you the most? Have you done any reading about it? If so, talk to each other about what you've learned. Would you ever like to travel there or move there to live temporarily?

SPEAK YOUR LOVE LANGUAGE

Buy your partner a gift from each of the places you visit on your trip. Remember acts of service when you're traveling, like helping with luggage or doing the check-ins at the airports.

MAKE THE MOST OF IT

Depending on your budget, make this date a tradition between the two of you. Whether it's once every few years or every few months, choose a new country to visit so that you can experience their pace of life, their time-honored traditions, their cuisine, and what makes them come together and celebrate.

DO NOT DISTURB
PASSPORT
SPF 50
DO NOT DISTURB
SPF 50
PASSPORT
DO NOT DISTURB
PASSPORT
SPF 50
DO NOT DISTURB

90

A TOURIST IN YOUR OWN TOWN

Chances are that there are many great attractions to see in your own city or hometown. But how often do you take the time to explore them as if you were a tourist? Well, now is your chance to tour and enjoy your city with fresh eyes on this bucket list date.

TIPS

- If your city is big enough, find a city tour to go on to see all the major highlights frequented by visitors.
- Map out your own tour ahead of time. Choose the landmarks you would like to explore.
- Take a lot of photos as you go along, then make them into a collage to put on your wall at home.

TALK ABOUT IT

Talk about what you find interesting or fascinating about each stop on your tour. Do some research on the history of your city and talk about what you find.

SPEAK YOUR LOVE LANGUAGE

Buy each other a little collection of memorable souvenirs throughout your day of playing tourist. Hold hands and put your arms around each other as you go strolling through the city. Walking can be tiring, so try to give each other a massage at the end of the day.

MAKE THE MOST OF IT

Book a hotel room and make a whole weekend of touring your city or hometown! You can get away from your day-to-day life and just focus on each other and exploring everything that your area has to offer.

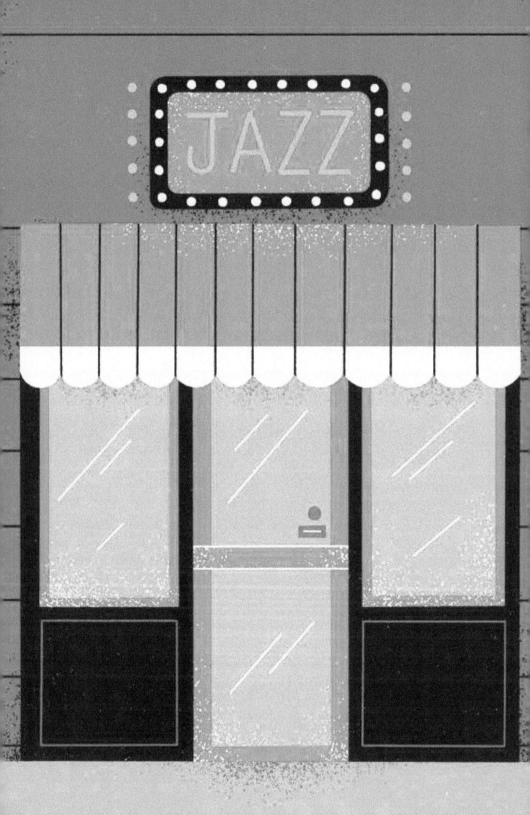

10

CLASSIC DATES

There's a reason why some dates are considered "classic," like dinner and a movie or a walk on the beach. They're easy to plan and experience, and we've found through our decades of modern courtship that they build connection, communication, and intimacy.

Whether you are just starting to date or have been together for a while, finding the time and energy to plan a unique date or experience with your partner can be difficult. That's why classic dates can be so useful.

For couples just starting out, these dates offer a tried-and-true template to help you build long-lasting resilience as a couple. For couples that have been together for longer, these dates can be a great way to restart a regular dating cadence and/or reignite the feelings you had when you first started dating. Date night matters, and it doesn't have to be "unique" or "extreme" to make a significant positive impact on your relationship.

Wherever you are in your relationship, remember that dating regularly is so important to maintaining and strengthening your partnership. The more you date, the happier you will be in your relationship over time. The correlation between date nights and relational happiness is very high and significant.

In this chapter, you will find "classic" dates. Some may have a bit of a twist to bring a little spice to your date nights.

91 DANCE WHERE NO ONE IS WATCHING

You don't need to go to the local club or take salsa dancing lessons to have a great date. You can just put on some music and make your living room into a dance floor! Dancing to music is the perfect way to stay connected—even in the privacy of your own home.

TIPS

- Before you start dancing, create a playlist together full of songs that you want to move your bodies to. This is both a bonding activity and a way to make sure you both get to hear your favorite songs on your date.
- Play your partner songs with lyrics that remind you of them.
- Dress up as if you were going to a wedding or formal event. This makes the date more special and different from everyday life.

TALK ABOUT IT

Talk about the first impressions you had of your partner when you met. What were your first thoughts? Were they positive or negative? How have those impressions changed over time (if at all)?

SPEAK YOUR LOVE LANGUAGE

Dancing with each other is an expression of affection through touch. When you play songs that remind you of your partner, explain why and tell them what you like or love most about them.

MAKE THE MOST OF IT

Pair the dancing with a romantic candlelit dinner. Buy champagne and flowers to decorate the "dance floor" in your home. Record some of your evening so that you can remember it in the future.

92 MARATHON MOVIE DATE

Most people watch movies on their couches these days, but it's time to liven up the movie date and be more creative.

TIPS

- Have a movie marathon day *at* the movies. Choose a few new releases currently playing in theaters, start as early in the day as you can, and stay as late as possible.
- Find a theater that offers a dining experience. You'll combine movies with food and cocktails and wonder if you can ever go back to watching movies any other way.
- Go to a drive-in movie theater. Yes, they still exist! And they're still absolutely wonderful!

TALK ABOUT IT

Between movies, talk about what you liked or didn't like. Was the plot intriguing? Did you expect the ending? If you could rewrite it yourself, how would you change it? Were there any characters that reminded you of your partner?

SPEAK YOUR LOVE LANGUAGE

Some theaters now offer couple's seats without an armrest between them, so see if you can sit in one of those so that you can comfortably hold hands. Whisper in your partner's ear during the movies and tell them something you adore about them (if they don't mind talking while watching!).

MAKE THE MOST OF IT

Make your own backyard movie theater. All you need is a portable projector, a laptop to connect it to, and a screen to project the image onto (a white bedsheet will do). This option gives you maximum control over your date: You can serve a romantic dinner, champagne, and a decadent dessert and play your favorite movies all cuddled up under the stars.

93

CAFÉ SPEED DATE

Life is busy for most people, so some days you may not even have the time to just sit, relax, and enjoy drinking coffee with your partner. This is your chance! Use this date for those times when your schedules never seem to connect. If sneaking in this café date is what helps you stay connected, intimate, and regularly dating, then it is "bucket-worthy." Find a coffee shop or café where you can relax for a short spell, talk over some coffee, and have some snacks.

TIPS

- Take your coffee to a nearby park or bench. That way, you can also enjoy nature along with your beverage.
- Even if you can only carve out 30 minutes for this café date, turn off your phones and be present with each other.
- Be old-fashioned and bring a newspaper or a magazine. Talk to each other about the news articles you find interesting.

TALK ABOUT IT

If this is a busy/hectic/stressful/challenging time, check in with each other. Ask your partner how they're doing, how work or school is going, and how you can help support them. Take a few minutes to plan your next full date.

SPEAK YOUR LOVE LANGUAGE

Sit next to each other at the café or on the park bench. Give your partner a long hug, and tell them how glad you are to see them, even for a short time.

MAKE THE MOST OF IT

Rather than stick to one tried-and-true spot for your café dates, find as many new places to meet as you can! These micro-dates can help you discover new areas of your town to enjoy.

94 MEET ME AT THE JAZZ CLUB

If you go out to listen to music on a date, it's probably usually at a place that plays pop music. Going to a jazz club, however, can bring a touch of old-world class to a familiar dinner date and perhaps introduce you to a new genre of music that you may end up loving.

TIPS

- If you're not familiar with jazz, take some time to listen to it together before your date so that you can appreciate it more.
- Because jazz reminds some people of the Roaring Twenties, dress up for your date and pretend that you've gone back in time!
- Instead of sipping on your normal cocktail, ask the bartender to recommend an unusual new drink to try.

TALK ABOUT IT

Since this date is all about the music, talk about what other genres of music you both like. What is your favorite and what is your least favorite? What are your favorite songs and why?

SPEAK YOUR LOVE LANGUAGE

In the spirit of the musical theme of this bucket list date, write your partner a song to express your feelings about them. Don't worry—you don't actually have to perform it (unless that's something you want to do). Just writing down the lyrics is romantic enough.

MAKE THE MOST OF IT

Dress up in the fashion of the 1920s and 1930s Jazz Age for your night out. If you find that you enjoyed your small taste of the era, consider taking lessons to learn popular dance moves from the Roaring Twenties, such as the Charleston or the foxtrot.

95 A NIGHT OF LAUGHS

There's nothing better in life than combining love with humor! Laughter is a great way to forget the stresses of life and take a more lighthearted view of things. It's also a wonderful way to bond with your partner.

TIPS

- Research the comedians at comedy clubs near you ahead of time so that you can choose who you want to see together.
- If you go to an early show, go out for drinks and music afterward. If you see the late show, then have dinner beforehand.
- Never heckle the comedians and don't talk during performances. These are rude behaviors that can throw the comedians off. Instead, cozy up to each other, listen, and laugh.

TALK ABOUT IT

Tell each other jokes before or after the show. What are the funniest jokes you've ever heard in your life? What are the worst ones? Challenge yourselves to make up a new joke together.

SPEAK YOUR LOVE LANGUAGE

Sit close to each other while you face the stage, and put your arms around each other or hold hands. Whisper sweet nothings into your partner's ear—tell them what you love about them and what you want to do with them after the show.

MAKE THE MOST OF IT

Instead of just going to one comedy show, find another live show of your choosing and go to a matinee. Try to find a comedic play, too. That way, you can make the whole day about laughing until your sides hurt!

96 MURDER MYSTERY DINNER THEATER

Gear up for a night of mystery, intrigue, and murder! Murder mystery dinner theaters are always fun because they immerse you in a thrilling whodunit experience with crazy characters and shady suspects. And the best part is—you get to play!

TIPS

- Many of these theaters encourage participants to dress up according to the theme of the show, so be creative and get into character.
- Work together as a team with your partner to try to solve the murder mystery.
- Reach out to other participants and try to figure things out together. You might even meet new friends!

TALK ABOUT IT

Have a conversation about your favorite thriller and murder mystery movies. Why do you like them so much? Are any of them predictable? Did you figure out the endings before they occurred?

SPEAK YOUR LOVE LANGUAGE

Sit next to each other and hold hands or put your arms around each other. Compliment your partner's costume for the evening, and praise them when they get clues right or if they figure out who the murderer is.

MAKE THE MOST OF IT

Have a contest to see who can identify the murderer first. After the show, go somewhere else to extend the evening. Do research ahead of time to try to find a restaurant or bar in your town that matches the era of your dinner theater experience. For example, if the show was set during the Jazz Age, perhaps you can find a themed speakeasy that brings you back to the Roaring Twenties.

97 CAMP OUT IN YOUR BACKYARD

Whether or not you are a camping enthusiast, you can have fun on this bucket list date! Buy or borrow a tent, set it up in your backyard, and pretend that you are camping. Stepping out of your normal routine is a refreshing way to shake up a date night.

TIPS

- If you can, buy a propane stove and cook a simple meal over it. Try to mimic a real camping mealtime experience.
- Set up an air mattress and put your sleeping bags on top of it for extra comfort.
- Light candles, play music, and drink some champagne while you hang out in your tent.

TALK ABOUT IT

Do you enjoy the outdoors? Did you ever go camping as a kid, or have you gone as an adult? Ask your partner if they've ever slept under the stars before. Spending time outdoors is a good way to reflect on one's relationship with nature.

SPEAK YOUR LOVE LANGUAGE

Lie down on your sleeping bags or air mattress and cuddle under the blankets. Look into each other's eyes and tell your partner what you are enjoying the most about them in the moment.

MAKE THE MOST OF IT

If you would rather go on a real camping experience, try venturing beyond your backyard. You could reserve a site at a campground, a state park, or your local woods. Maybe you'd even like to try renting a yurt and glamping!

98 A DAY AT SEA

Being on the water is always romantic, so rent a boat for the day and take to the sea (or lake). You could set sail on a speedboat, pontoon, rowboat, kayak, Jet Skis, sailboat, or any other watercraft that pleases you. Spend all day floating around with your partner and enjoying the fresh air.

TIPS

- Choose a boat with a radio or sound system so that you can listen to your favorite music. Try playing your favorite romantic playlist from your phone.
- Pack a lunch, snacks, and your favorite drinks. Turn off the boat and float around while you eat.
- Get a raft so that you can dock the boat on a sandbar, float in the water, and talk.

TALK ABOUT IT

Talk about your experiences with water. Was there ever a time when you were afraid of it? When did you first learn to swim? Did you go to waterparks or go boating when you were a kid?

SPEAK YOUR LOVE LANGUAGE

Put sunscreen on each other. If you float around on a raft(s), hold hands and stay close to each other. Compliment your partner on how sexy they look in their swimsuit.

MAKE THE MOST OF IT

If you decide to rent a ski boat or pontoon, then get adventurous. With water skis, inner tubes, and other similar equipment, you can have a day on the water that's not only romantic but also active.

99 FIELD TRIP DATE

When we grow to be adults, sometimes we forget to visit the kinds of places that we found so fascinating and fun as kids. Go on a date at the zoo, aquarium, or planetarium, and marvel at all the animals in our world and planets in our galaxy.

TIPS

- Take selfies of you and your partner standing in front of as many animals as you can at the zoo. Create an animal album of the two of you.
- If you go to the aquarium, have a contest with each other to find the most colorful fish possible.
- At the planetarium, be sure to attend a presentation so that you can look up into the dark "sky," watch the star projector, and learn more about our universe.

TALK ABOUT IT

Talk to each other about what you are seeing. What is your favorite animal and why? Which ones are the cutest and the scariest? Do you think there is life on other planets?

SPEAK YOUR LOVE LANGUAGE

Walk around these places, hold hands, and stay close to each other. Observe what your partner's favorite animal is, and go buy a stuffed animal of it at the gift shop. Be of service to each other as you plan the day by setting alarms on your phone for performance times or finding a map so that you don't get lost wandering.

MAKE THE MOST OF IT

Instead of just choosing one place (zoo, aquarium, or planetarium), visit all three! If you don't live in a big enough city to do that, then plan a weekend visit to somewhere that has all of them. Make it a fun trip to see as many sites and museums as you can.

100 DINNER CRUISE

While it's always fun to go out to a fancy dinner, it's even more exciting to do it on a yacht or riverboat! Dining on the water adds an extra layer of romance and intrigue. Plus, you have beautiful scenery to watch as you float around.

TIPS

- Decide what kind of cruise you would like to go on. Some have an old-school riverboat theme, while others are more modern.
- If the boat you choose has outdoor access, walk around the decks and go to the top so that you can feel the wind in your hair.
- Try to find a cruise that has a live band. Adding dancing to the evening is fun and romantic.

TALK ABOUT IT

If you have ever been on a cruise ship for a vacation, talk to each other about your favorite parts of the experience. If you haven't taken a cruise (or want to take another one), where would you want to go? Make a plan for going sometime in the near future.

SPEAK YOUR LOVE LANGUAGE

Buy your partner flowers (a boutonniere or a corsage) to wear as a gift, just like you might have on prom night when you were younger. As you walk around the decks, hold hands and put your arms around each other. Find a secluded spot to kiss for a few moments while you're alone.

MAKE THE MOST OF IT

If you don't live in an area that offers dinner cruises, make a short trip to a city that does. The dinner cruise can be one night of a mini-vacation that includes many other fun activities and exploration of another city.

101 SUPER DATE
MYSTERY TRIP TO NOWHERE

Sometimes the best plan is having no plan at all! Get into your car, start driving, and see where you end up. Stay on the look-out for fun places to get out, such as unique restaurants, thrift stores, historical monuments, or whatever you pass by.

TIPS

- At every light or intersection, flip a coin. If it lands heads, turn right. If it lands tails, turn left.
- Take turns driving. The passenger is the director and tells the driver where to turn and when to stop.
- Go as far as you possibly can. Turn onto streets you've never been on, or simply drive off into no-man's-land.

TALK ABOUT IT

Car trips are a great time to hold hands and talk. Tell each other stories about road trips you took as children. Talk about your favorite ones, why they were your favorites, and every-thing you can remember from them. Also, tell stories about your worst road trips—try to make them as funny as you can!

SPEAK YOUR LOVE LANGUAGE

Make a playlist for your partner full of all of their favorite songs. Hold hands and take turns listening to each other's playlists. At each stop, buy your partner a small gift to express your love; they should do the same for you.

MAKE THE MOST OF IT

Don't just spend a few hours doing this around your hometown. Go as far as you can for as long as you can, and see as many historical landmarks as you can. If you are really adventurous, you can even drive cross-country. Stay at any hotel or motel you happen to pass along the way.

DO NOT DISTURB
PASSPORT
SPF 50
DO NOT DISTURB
SPF 50
PASSPORT
DO NOT DISTURB
PASSPORT
SPF 50
DO NOT DISTURB

RESOURCES

Online Resources
Her Side His Side, https://HerSideHisSide.com
A relationship and dating website that gives advice from both male and female perspectives.

Inspiyr, Inspiyr.com
Articles on motivation, success, and self-improvement.

Lifehack, Lifehack.org
Covers a variety of topics, including relationships, communication, and self-improvement.

LovePanky, LovePanky.com
Gives a wide range of relationship advice, from romantic to adventurous.

Relationship Development and Transformation Magazine, Relationship-Development.com
A great resource for all kinds of dating and relationship advice.

Print Books
Daring Greatly: How the Courage to Be Vulnerable Transforms the Way We Live, Love, Parent, and Lead by Brené Brown
Examines the power of vulnerability and how to overcome fear of vulnerability in your relationship and life in general.

The Five Love Languages: How to Express Heartfelt Commitment to Your Mate by Gary Chapman
Gives an in-depth look at the five love languages and how to apply them to your relationship.

Getting the Love You Want: A Guide for Couples by Harville Hendrix and Helen LaKelly Hunt
Explains the psychology of love and how to apply it to your relationship.

Men Are from Mars, Women Are from Venus by John Gray
Lays out the main differences between men and women and how to understand each other.

Relationship Rescue: A Seven-Step Strategy for Reconnecting with Your Partner by Phillip C. McGraw
Helps you take personal responsibility for your relationship and gives tips on how to fix problems.

INDEX

ABOUT THE AUTHOR

 Dr. Carol Morgan is a relationship, dating, and success expert and a professor at Wright State University. She earned her PhD in Gender & Interpersonal Communication from the University of Nebraska.

In addition to her work as a teacher, she is a dating and relationship coach, speaker, and writer. She is the author of several books, including *Radical Relationship Resource: A Guide for Repairing, Letting Go, or Moving On* with best-selling author Dick Sutphen. She has also written hundreds of articles and appeared in videos for many popular websites, such as HuffPost, LovePanky, Lifehack, and eHow. Her articles have been shared on social media millions of times.

Dr. Carol is the owner of https://HerSideHisSide.com, a relationship and dating website that gives advice from both male and female perspectives. She also has created a video course entitled *How to Make a Man Love You . . . Even if You Don't Love Yourself* that teaches women how to love themselves and what to do to find and keep a quality partner.

She regularly appears as an expert on the TV show *Living Dayton* to share relationship and motivational advice. In addition, she has been a featured expert on DatingAdvice.com, Relationship Development and Transformation Magazine, and Inspiyr.

You can reach Dr. Carol through her websites: https://HerSideHisSide.com and DrCarolMorgan.com.